Praise for *Night Bloo*

D0483122

"Reading *Night Bloomers* is like having a dear friend right alongside you for support when most needed. Through stories, strategies, and writing prompts, Pearce provides powerful tools for building resilience, confidence, and joy. She reminds us that like plants, we don't bloom just once, as she gently, masterfully paves a path for us to enjoy a lifetime of growing and blossoming. A 'must-read' for anyone seeking some light in the darkness."

—**Caroline Welch,** CEO and co-founder of the Mindsight Institute and author of *The Gift of Presence: A Mindfulness Guide for Women*

"A gem of a book! Michelle Pearce has written an enlightening guide for anyone trying to find the path through a dark time in life. Through the wisdom gleaned from psychological research and practice and the lessons learned from her own personal encounter with pain and loss, Pearce points the way to growth and transformation when hope is in short supply. Down-to-earth, compassionate, and inspirational, *Night Bloomers* should be on everyone's bookshelf."

—**Kenneth I. Pargament, PhD,** author of *Spiritually Integrated Psychotherapy*

"Dr. Pearce's *Night Bloomers* is an essential guide on how to shift your perspective to find meaning in the mess that accompanies the crises in our lives. Filled with practical wisdom and easy-to-follow exercises, this book is sure to serve as a roadmap through and out of the darkness for all who find themselves on the journey of transformation."

—**Michelle Bailey, MD,** author of *Parenting Your Stressed Child*

"Michelle Pearce, PhD, is uniquely qualified to teach readers how to thrive in the face of grief in a way that captivates and illuminates. *Night Bloomers* is a therapeutic tool for healing based upon the transformative power of rewriting our stories of loss. *Night Bloomers* inspires readers to use sorrow as the soil in which to grow something beautiful."

—**Laura J. Oliver,** author of *The Story Within: New Insights and Inspirations for Writers*

"*Night Bloomers* shows how an intentional change in perspective and use of expressive writing exercises can bring hope and light, not at the end, but right in the middle of a dark tunnel. *Night Bloomers* is a sorely needed bright spot showing us the way to a happier, more hopeful life ahead.

—**Holly G. Prigerson, PhD,** Professor of Sociology in Medicine; Codirector, Cornell Center for Research on End-of-Life Care, Weill Cornell Medicine

"In *Night Bloomers*, Dr. Pearce offers a very practical, evidence-based, journaling approach to productively cope with the challenges of adversity. She uses her own personal adversity story and professional experiences as a psychologist to clearly outline steps and strategies to transform difficulties into transformation towards healing and resilience. A must-read for many trying to find a way out of the dark night of the soul and into some much needed light."

—**Thomas G. Plante, PhD, ABPP,** Professor and Director,
Applied Spirituality Institute, Santa Clara University

"Deeply insightful, heartfelt, practical, and wise, *Night Bloomers* is an indispensable resource for anyone who needs healing. Pearce does an eloquent and powerful job shifting our perspective on adversity and equipping us with the necessary tools to bloom in the dark. Anyone who has been through loss, grief, or times of adversity—or loves people who have—needs to read this book."

—**Harold G. Koenig, MD,** Professor of Psychiatry and Behavioral Sciences,
Duke University Medical Center

"Reading *Night Bloomers* is like having tea with your wisest, most loving friend who asks you tough questions with love and makes you think more deeply about every difficult experience. From purposely celebrating failures to knowing when to stop looking for more growth and just move on, this book is the perfect companion to shed wisdom and light on those dark nights of the soul."

—**Maggie Reyes,** host of The Marriage Life Coach Podcast
and author of *Questions for Couples Journal: 400 Questions to Enjoy,
Reflect, and Connect with Your Partner*

"A masterful guide for those wrestling with difficult situations. Not only does Dr. Pearce talk the talk, she has walked the walk. Her sincerity and deep knowledge of the topic are evident in every chapter. Her techniques allow you to change the lens when viewing your situation and give you tools so you can 'bloom.'"

—**Mary Lynn McPherson, PharmD, MA, MDE,**
Professor, Executive Director, Advanced Post-Graduate Education
in Palliative Care, Department of Pharmacy Practice and Science,
University of Maryland School of Pharmacy

NIGHT BLOOMERS

12 Principles
for
Thriving in Adversity

MICHELLE PEARCE, PhD

ixia
PRESS

Mineola, New York

Bibliographical Note

Night Bloomers: 12 Principles for Thriving in Adversity is a new work,
first published by Ixia Press in 2020.

Library of Congress Cataloging-in-Publication Data

Names: Pearce, Michelle, 1977– author.
Title: Night bloomers : 12 principles for thriving in adversity / Michelle
  Pearce, PhD.
Description: Mineola, New York : Ixia Press, [2020] | Includes bibliographical
  references. | Summary: "Loss, pain, and suffering are an inevitable part
  of the human experience. However, these circumstances can offer people
  opportunities for growth. Just as some flowers only bloom in the dark, so,
  too, some people require the darkness to bloom and become their best
  selves. Michelle Pearce, PhD, offers twelve practical tools for transforming
  loss and pain into positive growth and hope. In each chapter, she explains
  one of twelve empirically based principles of blooming in the dark, followed
  by writing prompts designed to help readers experience the principles in
  their own lives. In this hope-inspiring and compassionate guide, Dr. Pearce
  shares her clinical expertise and inspiring stories of other Night Bloomers
  to help individuals learn how to heal and transform their lives not in spite
  of their difficult times, but because of them."
Identifiers: LCCN 2019056137 | ISBN 9780486842370 (trade paperback)
Subjects: LCSH: Resilience (Personality trait) | Adjustment (Psychology) |
  Change (Psychology)
Classification: LCC BF698.35.R47 .P426 2020 | DDC 155.2—dc23
LC record available at https://lccn.loc.gov/2019056137

Ixia Press
An imprint of Dover Publications, Inc.

Manufactured in the United States by LSC Communications
84237101
www.doverpublications.com/ixiapress

2 4 6 8 10 9 7 5 3 1

2020

CONTENTS

CONTENTS

PREFACE

On a warm North Carolina October afternoon, I married the love of my life in a rose garden. Surrounded on all sides by thousands of roses in every color, it was one of the most amazing, love-filled, and picturesque moments of my life. How could I have known then that these gorgeous blooms were harbingers of the pain and despair—and later the beauty—that was to come?

I spent my second wedding anniversary alone, not knowing where my husband had gone for the day. It seemed that his work had become more important to him than me, and that had caused a lot of tension between us. When he finally came home that night, he told me that I was not his soulmate and that he didn't think we should have married. After many tears and a long conversation where we tried to sort things out, he surprised me by driving us to the rose garden where we had married. Perhaps this was a sort of apology gesture on his part.

It was nighttime by then, and I walked slowly, alone, between the rows of roses in the dark. The lattices were several feet taller than me, forming a maze of colorful blooms. The fragrance seemed richer than on the day we were married. Later I would read somewhere that the fragrance of roses is 40 percent more intense at night. I remember the deliciously magical feel of the garden in the moonlight and the buttery softness of the petals I couldn't help touching as I walked by. I noticed that many of the roses were curled up tight in a bud for the night, but some of the roses were still wide open, in full bloom. It made me think about how much beauty—how much life—can exist even under a veil of darkness.

A year later, my marriage and my life would be plunged into darkness and I would have the choice that each of those roses faced that night: to open up to life in the dark or to shut my eyes and close myself off from the pain. The best decision I ever made was to bloom in the dark. I want to help you make the same decision, regardless of the type of loss you have experienced, and reap the same rewards.

Not "Why," but "What Now?"

If you are anything like me, you've grown tired of people telling you that God or the universe has a purpose for the pain you are experiencing. I don't disagree with this concept. In fact, the message of this book is built upon this very idea. However, I had gotten weary of what I perceived to be a trite response. It seemed like they said it more for their peace of mind than for mine. It felt like being given a Band-Aid for an enormous, gaping wound. It just wasn't enough.

After my husband left, I would ask myself "why?" in hundreds of desperate ways: Why wasn't I good enough? Why didn't God intervene and make him come back? Why weren't any of my efforts to win him back working? I spent countless hours in therapy, journaling, praying, and speaking with friends, trying to understand why my husband had left. I thought doing so would help me figure out the purpose of the pain I was experiencing over my loss. I also thought I needed to fully understand why this situation had happened before I could begin to accept that it had happened. But instead of revealing the reason for my loss or the purpose of the pain, asking these "why" questions only led me deeper and deeper into despair and hopelessness.

There can certainly be wisdom and maybe some relief in understanding what leads to a painful experience. In my case, if I could identify how or what I had contributed to our breakdown, I could then work diligently to address the issues and not to repeat the mistakes. After many, many months of agonizing, I finally realized the "why" wasn't nearly as important as the "what now?" Eventually, it was the "what now?" that helped me to transform my pain into healing and new growth.

Don't Waste Your Sorrows

A friend gave me more than a Band-Aid one day when she sent me a quote from the well-known reverend and scholar, Dr. Timothy Keller: "How you respond to the troubles in your life will go a long way toward whether or not you ever, ever, ever develop courage, ever develop patience, ever develop compassion, ever develop sobriety and humility, ever develop any of those things. Don't waste your sorrows."

This created a significant change in my perspective. I had been living like a person driving a car with my eyes fixed on the rearview mirror: "What happened to my marriage?! Why, even with my best efforts, could I not fix it?" These obsessive questions and this way of viewing my situation were setting me up for a big crash. It was time to let go of the whys and start focusing on the more important questions: How was I going to move on? Who did I want to become as a result? And, what did I want my life to look like going forward?

Dr. Keller's words illuminate the purpose of our pain. Troubles are opportunities to become more—more courageous, more patient, more compassionate, more humble. We cannot develop these or other essential character virtues without going through a situation that calls for their use. For someone to call you patient, you must demonstrate patience. That means at some point you will have to wait for something, and likely that waiting will cost you something. Certainly it will cost you time, but often waiting costs us much more than that. To be told that you are courageous means you will have to face something that is scary and uncertain. To be called humble you will have to give up something, such as recognition that was due to you.

You see, it's not the trouble that causes us to become better people. Participating in life makes trouble inevitable, and not everyone comes out the other side in a better state. We all go down one of three roads when we encounter trouble. Trouble can destroy us. Trouble can leave us unchanged. Or, trouble can help to transform us. It takes conscious work and determination to choose to be transformed in the midst of trouble.

We do not need to seek out suffering so that we can become "more." I dislike suffering as much as the next person, and I would never have willingly chosen the painful events that have occurred in my life. What I'm saying is that if we're experiencing trouble and suffering, we have been given an opportunity. What we do with this opportunity is up to us.

To become "more" as a result of the suffering, we have to choose carefully and dig deep to figure out how we should best respond to our situation. We need to look at each sorrow as something we can use to spur regrowth. That's what Keller means when he says "don't waste your sorrows." I wanted my sorrow to end as quickly as possible. I spent a long time thinking that the only way to end my sorrow was for my husband to return and for us to go on with our lives together. If he would just see this as I did, come to his senses, and return home, then this terrible pain would end and I could go back to feeling like a normal human being. I would pray many times a day for this to happen. It never did.

Eventually, I realized that there was no easy way for this pain to be lifted from me, no matter how much I prayed and wept and tried to woo him back. I was going to have to move through this suffering, one moment at a time. Peering at the weeks and months and years that lay ahead of me, none of which included the man I loved, was terrifying. Would this suffering go on forever? I could see no end in sight. I wanted to know the most efficient path through the suffering. If I was going to have to endure this, then I at least wanted to know the shortest, least painful route through. But the more I tried to exert some sort of control over the suffering, the more intense it became.

I knew I had to stop driving looking through the rearview mirror. Keller's words haunted me. Don't waste your suffering. I don't like to waste anything. I have Christmas wrapping paper and ribbons that I have reused for the last fifteen years! I reuse Ziploc bags, water bottles, and tinfoil. I milk that toothpaste tube for every last drop of paste. If I had to work hard to earn the money to buy these things, then I want to get my money's worth.

Find Your Treasures in the Dark

I had to learn how to apply this same principle of not wasting anything to the situation in my marriage and the suffering I was experiencing. I had not been given a choice about the suffering I was experiencing, but I did have a choice about how I responded to it. In the chapters to come, I will tell you about the steps I took to more positively deal with my pain; how I restored my mental health and positive outlook; and how I used my difficult and sad experience to my benefit, creating an inspiring and meaningful identity and life for myself. I'll also tell you the blooming stories of some of my psychotherapy clients and Writing for Wellness workshop participants who experienced beauty and transformation as a result of the choices they made in the dark times in their lives. Each of us took deliberate steps, based on the principles I will outline in this book, to find our treasure and experience transformation.

As a result of the steps I took, so much good has happened in me and to me. I became a dancer and an author, two lifelong dreams of mine. I've traveled to Mexico, Italy, Cuba, and Israel by myself. I've returned to dating and learned a lot about myself and what kind of partner might be an excellent fit for me. I've become more flexible, relaxed, and confident. I've taken risks and essentially "came out of hiding." I've become a better therapist and friend. I'm more grateful and feel that I love people better, including myself. I'm clearer about my mission in life, and am having a lot more fun as I carry it out. I'd like to offer you the same process and tools I used, as have many of my clients, to help you experience wholeness and restoration, regardless of the type of loss or suffering you may be enduring.

I know you didn't choose to be in your current state. There is likely nothing fair about it. And, if you're like most of us, the only way out is through it. While you are in the midst of it, I offer you the hope that there are treasures waiting for you along this dark, painful path. Treasures that will enrich your life and equip you for what is up ahead. Treasures that can only be found in the dark. These treasures require you to embark on an intentional process of changing your thinking and your approach to adversity. Like Keller, I urge you to make a decision not to waste your sorrows or spend endless time looking in the rearview mirror. The choice you have is the same as the flowers each had in the rose garden that night—to open up to life in the dark or to shut your eyes and close yourself off from the pain. My hope is that you choose to bloom in the dark, and that the blooming principles and writing exercises in this book help you navigate your time in the darkness, allowing you to find your treasures and move through suffering into healing and wholeness.

—Michelle Pearce, fellow Night Bloomer

WRITING YOURSELF THROUGH THE DARK AND INTO A NEW PERSPECTIVE

What the caterpillar calls the end of the world,
the master calls a butterfly.

—RICHARD BACH

"Look at it again," my Psychology 101 professor urged us. I stared hard at the image on the screen, squinted, turned my head from side to side, even closed one eye and then the other, but still all I could see was an ugly, old woman.

"Watch," he said with a gleam in his eye, as he began to trace the outline of the image. This is a chin, not a nose, this is an ear, not an eye, her necklace, not her mouth. And then I saw her, the beautiful young lady that just a moment ago had been an ugly old woman. The topic of the class was on how our perception determines our reality. In this case, the famous picture on the screen contained two images—called a perceptual illusion—and depending on how you looked at it, the brain would interpret the picture as either an old woman or a young lady.

I was both fascinated and disturbed by how easy it was for me to miss something right before my eyes simply because my brain didn't know it was there, didn't know it was an option. I much preferred the image of the young lady, but until my brain had been instructed to see it, my reality was the old woman.

Your Perspective Determines Your Reality

The lesson that perception determines reality is a critical one, particularly for moving effectively through the inevitable pain and suffering in life. The way we look at things matters. It changes not only what we see, but also what we think, how we feel, what options and possibilities are available to us, how we relate to others and to ourselves, and whether we feel hope or despair. As a clinical psychologist, one of the greatest gifts I can give my clients is a change in perspective. Gaining a new perspective changes everything! One of the best compliments I have ever received was from a client at the end of treatment. When we first met, Tom had been bound up in rage, guilt, and despair over a violent hate crime that had been committed against him. He had been beaten by a stranger in broad daylight as he and his partner were walking along the street. He sustained a serious traumatic brain injury that left him deaf in one ear, and he was experiencing severe brain fog, memory and concentration problems, and a deep depression. When he came to see me, he was on medical leave from his job as a surgeon where for years he had provided skilled care for high-risk patients.

I explained to him the blooming in the dark metaphor on which this book is based. I still remember the look on his face of both astonishment and then hope when I shared this new perspective on trauma and loss. Over the next few months, we used the blooming perspective to help him work through his pain and find new meaning, a new narrative, and a new direction for his life. His depression resolved and so did his rage. He was able to forgive his attacker and even confront him with love and grace in the courtroom. Not only was he able to work, but he also decided to move to the part of the country he'd always wanted to live. He found a wonderful new home and job there, and he moved with his partner shortly after we finished to begin his new life. He radiated hope and joy. After thanking me for the work we had done together, he looked at me and said, "You know what, you're the 'real' Spin Doctor." Then he told me I needed to write this book, so that others could experience the same kind of transformation he did.

You most likely have a well-developed perspective on the difficult situation you are experiencing. You know your pain like the back of your hand. It might feel like it's going to be your reality for the rest of your life. I'm here to tell you that as awful as you feel right now and as permanent as this pain might feel, there is another option, another view of your pain and suffering through a different lens. With this new perspective comes a different way of being in your situation, of moving through your suffering, and even of enjoying your life again. Just like with the old lady/young lady perceptual illusion, once you see the other option available to you, you can never go back to not seeing it. That said, you may still prefer the first image you saw because sometimes it feels easier to stay in our current viewpoint—it's familiar and it's a path you have tread numerous times.

This book is intended to show you how to see another picture, another possible perspective on your current situation. It's also intended to give you effective, practical tools to move through your pain using this new perspective. Those two things—illuminating the new perspective and providing the practical tools—that's my job and my expertise. What you choose to do with this change in perspective and the tools is up to you.

Your Darkness Is Also Your Opportunity

When the darkness in life descends upon us, regardless of its source or type, it feels like the end of the world. The pain can become so intense that you long for the end of the world, or at least the end of your world of pain. I don't know specifically what you've been through or what you're going through now, but if the description of this book resonated with you, then it's likely that you will benefit from the blooming principles and exercises offered here. You are most likely at a place where your life will never be the same again and *you* will never be the same again. No amount of wishing or foot-stomping or crying or even praying will make things go back to how they were before your found yourself in this darkness. Your way of being has come to an end, and accepting this is one of our hardest tasks. We have to begin to trust that something greater is at work, and that something greater lies ahead.

I've come to believe that the darkness affords us a unique opportunity to radically change our lives and our identities and to find or change our life's purpose. It doesn't happen automatically. The darkness is an opportunity for transformation, not a guarantee. My goal is to help you take full advantage of this unique time in your life. My hope is that you use your difficult experience to find a new perspective and fulfilling life path.

I'm not going to tell you it's going to be all roses (pun intended)—there is real work to do in the dark. If your process is anything like mine and that of the clients I've worked with, it's going to be painful and messy and you're going to want out of the suffering. Badly. But if you're anything like those of us who have tread through this, you're going to gradually see how your painful situation will open up otherwise unavailable opportunities for self-awareness, greater meaning, and personal and spiritual growth.

I've Been There

I've had a number of those "life-turned-upside-down-and-smashed-into-tiny-pieces-and-I'm-not-sure-I'm-going-to-make-it" moments. Besides my parents' divorce, years struggling with a medically confusing chronic illness that leaves me profoundly fatigued, and a long-standing estrangement with my mother that saddens me to this day, I grieved hard over the loss of my marriage. When my husband left, all I could see was the death of my dreams, and I felt like I was dying. There were days when I wasn't sure I wanted to go on. I could not see beyond what I had lost. It was much easier to keep looking back with regret and sink into hopelessness and despair. I did everything I could think of to resurrect my past and restore my marriage. Nothing worked. The shame piled on as I helped other couples in my clinical practice through their marital difficulties and yet I couldn't fix my own.

It wasn't until I changed my perspective that I was able to see this time in my life in a much more positive light. Instead of seeing the mandatory year of separation before the divorce as a year to win my husband back, I began to see that I was being given time to build a whole new kind of outlook and life for myself. After the angst and mourning over my previous life, it was time to attend to me. During this time I would do more than heal; I would become more than I had ever been and my life would be set on an incredible new course.

My healing came when I realized that what I really needed was for my life, not my marriage, to be rejuvenated. I needed to become a woman who engaged courageously in life, who broke out of her routines and her self-limiting beliefs. I needed to become a woman who loved much and loved well. I had to stop letting fear control my life and my relationships. I needed to create and enjoy a richer and more joy-filled life. What I didn't realize and didn't want to do was give up my old way of being, my old perspective on life to get there. Yet, something must always die before resurrection. I needed to accept that my old way of living and my marriage were part of the past and that it was only *because* they were in the past that I could experience a new life and a broader perspective.

I am writing as one who has been where you are right now. I know how devastating it is to have your life, your marriage, your health, your family, and your dreams ripped from you and your heart torn into pieces. When I talk about this new perspective, I am in no way downplaying your pain. It's real and it's miserable. But that's not all it has to be. Let me tell you about the day when my perspective on my pain and loss changed.

Night Bloomers

I was in the clinic seeing clients one Wednesday afternoon not too long after my husband left. In those early days, it was hard to concentrate on what my clients were saying. My grief and fear were overshadowing everything in my life, including my work, which I loved. Over the lunch hour that day, I checked my phone and found a text message from a friend. She had sent me a picture of a vibrant pink flower with a message that read, "Night blooming cactus. I've cared for this cactus for years and it finally bloomed last night."

Those two sentences and that pink flower changed everything.

I had no idea that some flowers bloom in the dark, that some flowers actually *require* the dark to bloom. As I paused to consider this new information, it hit me: some *people* need the dark to bloom. Some people need the trials and suffering and loss and life upheavals to experience growth and transformation, to come into the fullness of their beings and life purpose. I am one of those people. Like it or not, my greatest personal growth has always come from spending a season in the darkness of pain, loss, and suffering. I think there are a lot of us out there who need the dark. I call us "Night Bloomers." If you're reading this book, there's a good chance that you or someone you love is a Night Bloomer. I wanted to write this book to provide my fellow Night Bloomers with hope. Hope that your heart-wrenching, faith-shaking loss may provide the fertile covering of darkness that can produce beauty not possible in the light.

A Famous Night Bloomer: From Prison to the Palace

To help you get an idea of what I'm talking about, let me tell you a story about someone who chose to bloom in the dark. Nelson Mandela (1918–2013) has been described as a protester, a prisoner, a president, and a peacemaker. I would add to that list a Night Bloomer. Mandela, who grew up in a small village called Transkei in South Africa, knew what it was like to suffer. He knew what it was like to lose things that were important to him. He lost his eldest son, his two grandchildren, his freedom, and his ability to control his life. He lost twenty-seven years with his wife and family while he sat in a dark prison cell.

Mandela had a strong sense of justice. He fought against racial oppression. To many he was a saint and a hero, but Mandela wasn't always this way. In the 1950s, he was number one on South Africa's terrorist list, as the founder of a military wing of the African National Congress. Although he fought for human rights, originally there were groups of people he did not want to include in this fight, such as Indians.

Listen to how Richard Stengel, who collaborated with Mandela on his autobiography, *Long Walk to Freedom*, describes how prison changed Mandela:

> "The man who went into prison in 1962 was hotheaded and easily stung. The man who walked out into the sunshine of the mall in Cape Town twenty-seven years later was measured, even serene … I asked him many times during our weeks and months of conversations what was different about the man who came out of prison compared to the man who went in, he finally sighed and then said simply, 'I came out mature.'"

Prison was where Nelson Mandela bloomed in the dark. We remember Mandela not as the man before prison, or the man in prison, but as the man he was after he emerged from prison. He prevented a devastating racial civil war and created a democratic South Africa. His life had an astounding impact on human tolerance and freedom, not only in South Africa, but all around the world. The first president of a democratic South Africa, champion of the anti-apartheid fight, bestower of dignity to the poor, and Nobel Peace Prize laureate had bloomed in the dark. The hard work of these achievements was done while he sat in that dark, lonely prison cell for twenty-seven years, refusing to allow the suffering and injustice to destroy him.

Mandela could not have negotiated peace as an angry man. The personal transformation he went through in prison allowed him to complete the mission ahead of him. He needed the softening that comes from choosing over and over again to extend grace and forgiveness to your oppressors. In his fight for human justice, he had to be strong, but not revengeful; courageous, but not cocky. He had to forgive, but not compromise. These are the lessons he learned in prison. These are the blossoms that required the dark to grow and mature. The world will forever be a better place because Mandela chose to bloom.

An Everyday Night Bloomer

Ok, so we're not all going to be Nelson Mandelas. Let me share with you another real-life example, lest you think this paradigm shift is only for a highly select few. This story is about my friend and colleague, Jenny Owens, who did something remarkable after she and her husband nearly lost their newborn son. I'll let Jenny tell the story in her own words:

> "In April of 2016, my husband and I were thrilled to welcome our son Maximus Owens to the world. Within hours of his birth, Max was diagnosed with a rare condition called congenital diaphragmatic hernia. His diaphragm was not fully formed at birth, allowing his bowels to move into his chest cavity, displacing his heart and crushing and impacting the development of his left lung. The doctors gave Max a 50 percent chance of survival and it was a very rough start the first few months as Max and physicians fought for his life. He spent several weeks in the NICU and more time in the children's hospital as he underwent several surgeries.

"When we were staying at the hospital for one of Max's surgeries, I ran into a grandmother of an infant patient in the family lounge. We chatted for a while, and during our conversation she shared that she was visiting for two weeks and staying at a hotel. Her son and daughter were living in a tiny hospital room at the Children's Hospital until either the Children's House or Ronald McDonald House had an open room. They were from Tennessee and had traveled all the way to Baltimore for specialists that could care for their baby's rare condition. They would be there for months while their tiny baby had multiple surgeries.

"Right then I realized how incredibly lucky we were to be in Baltimore and so close to such amazing hospitals. Had we lived in a more rural area, Max may not have had access to the critical treatment he needed for survival, especially since we weren't aware of his life-threatening condition before birth. When we were in the NICU we could get home in ten minutes, but many families traveled hours to be there each day and stayed months longer than we did. I thought about it all night and most of our stay. And I wondered—what if people living nearby hospitals could volunteer rooms in their homes to people traveling with loved ones for care?"

In 2016, Jenny started a nonprofit organization in Baltimore, Maryland, called Hosts for Humanity. The organization matches volunteer hosts with patient families seeking a place to stay while their loved ones receive care. Family and friends of patients now have a low-cost and supportive place to stay while their loved one is in the hospital.

I spoke with Jenny again recently about the idea of blooming in the dark and here's what she said:

"Reflecting over the last couple of years, I've experienced periods of both extreme highs and crushing lows. I felt lowest when Max's first surgery failed a few weeks after his birth. When the surgery team rolled him into the room and triumphantly declared a successful repair, I didn't feel their elation. I felt despair. I didn't see a newborn that had been "successfully repaired," but instead one that was hopped up on fentanyl, puffy, and nonresponsive. I wanted to lie on the floor, for no other reason than my body seemed to want to reflect my emotional state. Fast forward almost two years, and Max is now a thriving and resilient toddler. We feel tremendous gratitude for his health, and for an amazing support network that took care of us when we were down. And although pain in all its forms is a state I don't want to be in for long, I've come to appreciate it for facilitating a journey of tremendous personal growth.

"Some pain is unavoidable, systemic, or just bad luck—perhaps a car accident, an illness. Some pain you play a part in, by neglecting your health, finances, relationships, etc. I try to see pain as a sophisticated alert system identifying a credible threat. Pain told me to "pay attention!" loudly and forcefully. So I did. After I witnessed the need for housing I could no longer do nothing. This suffering showed me the hidden pain of others, and radically altered the path of my life."

Jenny could have spent the year after her son was born simply cherishing her time with him and her husband (and I know she did a lot of that). She could have gotten stuck in her trauma and fear and anger. But through hard work, determination, and the love and support of others, Jenny took her pain and fear and turned it into something incredible, an organization that helps others who are experiencing similar pain and fear. Jenny said she never would have thought of doing something like this until she experienced this kind of suffering. She wouldn't have seen the need, wouldn't have felt the same pull on her heart. The world is a better place because Jenny experienced this pain and allowed herself to use it to help others. She's an inspiration. She's a Night Bloomer.

A Change in Perspective Changes Everything

My hope is that this metaphor—flowers and people who *require* the dark to bloom—has begun to shift your perspective from one of loss and despair to one of growth and hope. Because once you change your perspective, you can begin to use your own inner resources and creativity to begin moving in this new life-affirming direction.

Let me just pause to clear something up before we build on the new perspective and guiding metaphor of the book: Blooming in the dark is *not* about whether what got you into the dark—perhaps the death of a loved one, divorce, illness, abuse, loss of physical functioning, a fractured relationship, a child addicted to drugs, job loss, or bankruptcy—was good or right. None of these things are good. And debatably none of them are "right." Nor does this metaphor mean that we should purposely pursue or create painful situations in our lives so that we can grow. Rather, the message of blooming in the dark is that *the dark presents us with a unique opportunity that if harnessed skillfully can propel a life forward in ways that couldn't occur if the darkness had never happened.*

I've designed this book as a guide to help you view your particular situation in a new way and to equip you with effective and powerful tools, so that you can navigate the darkness in your life skillfully. I will share with you principles about blooming that I have learned from practicing psychotherapy for nearly two decades. I will tell you about some of the empirical findings I have learned as a researcher who studies coping with stressors and who develops interventions to improve mental health. I will share transformative knowledge that as a university faculty member I teach my students about integrative health and wellness, such as mind-body approaches for healing, including journal writing. I'll provide many of the powerful writing prompts I've used as a Writing for Wellness workshop facilitator with people who want to process and grow from cancer and chronic illness. And I'll share some of the strategies I use as a health and wellness coach when I assist individuals in achieving goals they thought were beyond their reach.

I will also share with you the exciting findings of many other researchers that support the blooming principles in this book, so that you can feel confident that the tools we'll be using are effective. But beyond all this professional experience and research, I will also meet you in these pages as a fellow Night Bloomer. You'll witness part of my personal journey, as well as those of some of my clients and workshop participants, and even those of some famous individuals who bloomed in the dark. I see myself as a humble guide with hard-won experience, a guide who has traversed this path many times before with people from all walks of life and who has learned some of the secrets of finding treasures and experiencing transformation in the dark.

Psychiatrist Viktor Frankl, a Holocaust survivor, asserted that "suffering ceases to be suffering … at the moment it finds a meaning." Indeed, despite the old adage that "time heals all wounds," recent research shows that the real healer is "finding meaning"[1]. The goal of *Night Bloomers* is to help you make meaning out of your suffering, so that the darkness in which you find yourself can become a fruitful time of healing and personal growth. Now, let's turn our attention to why writing is such a powerful tool for blooming in the dark.

To me alone, there came a thought of grief:
A timely utterance gave that thought relief
And I again am strong.

—WILLIAM WORDSWORTH, 1807

Writing Is Good for You

Early on in my graduate studies, I came across a series of research papers describing how writing can help people feel better emotionally and physically. I did a deep dive into the literature and was fascinated with what I found. Dr. James Pennebaker is considered the pioneer in expressive writing, or as it's called in the research, written disclosure. Little did I know then that ten years later he would train me how to lead Writing for Wellness workshops. In Pennebaker's original writing experiment in 1986, now repeated hundreds of times by researchers around the world, he and his team asked undergraduate students to write about either a trauma or a neutral topic (such as describing the room they were sitting in) for fifteen to twenty minutes a day over a period of four days[2]. The students who wrote about a trauma, describing both the traumatic event and their feelings about it, experienced better physical health, fewer doctor visits, improved sleep, less pain, and more positive mood over the following months. That was our first glimpse that there was something about getting one's pain into the written word that helps the body and mind feel better.

Since then, researchers have found a host of other benefits for the writer[3], including better immune system functioning by stimulating T-helper cell growth and antibody response to viruses and vaccinations[4], improved wound healing[5], lower pain levels[6], better sleep[7], and lower cortisol levels[8], blood pressure, and heart rate[9]. Writing has also been shown to improve our emotional and psychological well-being[10], including increasing positive affect[11] and reducing depression[12], anxiety[13], post-traumatic stress[14], and intrusive thoughts and avoidance, which are associated with the experience of trauma[15]. The physiological changes facilitated by writing cause our bodies and minds to relax, creating a fertile context for healing.

The benefits have gone beyond health. Research has also found that those who have written about emotional topics experienced better grades, found jobs more quickly, and were absent from work less often compared to those who did not write about emotional topics[16].

The Type of Writing Matters

Some of you might be thinking that writing about your worst trauma or whatever has landed you in the dark will increase your distress, just like thinking or talking about it can make you feel worse. And you'd be right, but only partially so. Researchers have found that some people who write about a distressing topic tend to feel worse after they finish writing compared to people who write about neutral topics[17]. The good news is that this outcome changes over time: The initial distress after writing about stressors and trauma is short-lived and for many turns into long-term positive changes in emotional well-being. Not so for those who write about neutral topics. They don't experience positive changes in their emotional well-being.

Other fascinating research has shown that the type of writing matters. People who experience *intrusive* rumination—distressing thoughts that just pop into your head and run on an endless negative or catastrophic loop—are more likely to experience post-traumatic stress disorder, a debilitating condition that can occur after experiencing a trauma[18]. However, people who engage in *deliberate* rumination—intentionally thinking about a distressing event in a particular way—are more likely to experience post-traumatic growth, or positive effects as a result of experiencing a trauma or stressor.

Both intrusive and deliberate rumination involve repetitive thinking. The difference is that deliberate thinking is an intentional process to examine and reflect on a situation. This type of repetitive thinking is good for us. It helps us create meaning, reduce fear, and change unhelpful thinking styles[19]. We can use carefully crafted writing prompts to facilitate this type of deliberate, repetitive thinking. These types of writing prompts provide us with a time-focused, intentional rumination experience about our adversity. This leads to meaning-making and new healing narratives, which ultimately sets us up for post-traumatic growth.

After discovering this compelling research on expressive journal writing, I started using writing in my work with clients as an activity they could do between sessions. Many of them benefited from this writing. After receiving training with Dr. Pennebaker at Duke University, I then began offering Writing for Wellness workshops for students, community members, and people who were going through or had gone through the experience of cancer and chronic illness. The feedback on the helpfulness of writing was so encouraging that it motivated me to keep coming up with new prompts for expressing our deepest thoughts and feelings and for facilitating transformation. What my clients and workshop participants were experiencing mirrored what the research has found over the last thirty-plus years: writing helps people who are suffering.

Writing Was My Lifeline

And then the research got real. When my husband left, and like I have done in every other crisis, I pulled out my journal and started writing. Every evening before bed, I would look forward to the twenty or thirty or even sixty minutes I had to pour out my heart on the page, relieved that I wasn't exhausting anyone by saying the same things over again or expressing the same pain that I thought I should have been over by now. Some days, I'd even take a ten-minute break at work to just write about what I was thinking and feeling—a lifeline for those first few months of foggy sadness.

On the sage advice of my writing coach, I turned my journaling into a memoir, chronicling the year of separation up to the day in court when a judge granted the divorce. I would write a chapter and then edit it, write another and edit it, and so on until the book was complete. Then I edited the whole book several times. With every revision, I found myself getting stronger and happier. It wasn't until I finished the book that I realized I had just done the equivalent of trauma therapy, which is telling your trauma story again and again until it loses its emotional power; has a beginning, middle, and most importantly an end; and gets integrated into your entire life story.

I knew I was through the darkness when my divorce story was just a chapter in my life story and not my entire life story, which is how it felt when I was in the middle of it. Interestingly, as I did more research for this book, I came across a study that showed that among recently separated adults, creating a narrative about their divorce experience seemed to be the most helpful type of writing for emotional recovery[20].

Writing Can Help You Too

We're going to use writing as our primary tool for blooming. Writing will allow you to move through your suffering by first acknowledging its existence and then processing it. We'll use writing to release your painful emotions and dark thoughts rather than ruminating on them continuously[21]. But to heal, you'll need to do more than simply recall your story; you'll need to reconstruct your story[22]. To reconstruct your experience through writing, you'll use the writing prompts in the following chapters to search for and find meaning in your suffering— what are the lessons to be learned, the benefits to be experienced, the resolution necessary to move forward? We'll also use writing to explore other perspectives, identities, and pathways to wholeness that will facilitate greater ease as you move through the dark.

You'll find that as you write your story, it will become more objective and you will gain emotional distance from it. Eventually, you will integrate the trauma and suffering into your overall life narrative, so that it no longer runs the show. Like editing, you will "rework and reword," and finally you will write a new ending to your story. I will guide you through each of these steps using the prompts in the pages to come.

How to Use This Book

Here are a few things you should know and do before we get started:

* *Twelve Principles of Blooming in the Dark.* This book is organized
  around twelve principles of blooming in the dark. These are
  principles I learned through my own seasons in the dark and those
  of my clients. Each principle and accompanying writing prompt is
  grounded in empirical research from various domains of psychology.
  One chapter is devoted to each principle. Following the description
  of each blooming principle, there are six to eight thought-provoking
  journaling prompts for you to complete at a pace that feels right to
  you. These prompts are designed to help you experience each of the
  twelve principles of blooming in the dark.

* *Choose a beautiful blooming journal.* If you haven't already done so,
  find a lined journal in which to respond to the writing prompts
  in this book. It should be a journal that inspires you to write.
  Maybe the cover is your favorite color or has a background you
  find inspiring. I'd recommend you begin with a new journal
  rather than one you've already written in, so that it can be devoted
  exclusively to your blooming process. If you'd find it easier to have
  the writing prompts already typed into your journal, I've created
  a downloadable PDF that lists each of the writing prompts for
  the twelve blooming principles with lots of blank space after
  each prompt. You can find *My Night Blooming Journal* at www.
  drmichellepearce.com/nightbloomersjournal

* *You do not need to be a writer to benefit from this book and the journal
  exercises.* The writing exercises in *Night Bloomers* are designed
  for personal transformation, not to sharpen grammar, spelling, or
  composition skills. In fact, paying attention to those aspects of writing
  can impede the effectiveness of using writing as a tool for healing.

* *It doesn't matter what type of pain and suffering you're going through, this book is for you.* The twelve blooming principles and the writing prompts I've designed are applicable to many different "dark times" in life, such as loss, grief, death, illness, divorce, breakups, job loss, aging parents, estrangement, miscarriage, rape, assault, bankruptcy, affairs, disability, life transitions and upheavals, and so on.

* *You can work through the twelve blooming principles and accompanying prompts at your own pace.* Some of you may complete the journal exercises in a few weeks, others in a few months, while others may take even longer than that. The important thing is to go at a pace that keeps you growing.

* *Be sure to keep watering your seed through your writing even when you don't see signs of growth.* If it feels like too much to work through all the chapters and prompts in order, you can dip in and out of the chapters. There are also enough writing prompts in each chapter that you can choose the ones that most resonate. You can also go back and complete prompts you didn't complete earlier or respond to prompts again, once you are further along in the process and your responses might have evolved.

* *Writing might make you feel a little worse before it makes you feel better.* In the research, some participants reported feeling more distress for an hour or two after writing about a traumatic event. However, over time the people who wrote about a trauma—and not the people who wrote about a neutral event—experienced better emotional and physical health[23].

* *This is different from your childhood diary.* The prompts are designed to help you reflect, find meaning, discover new perspectives, glean insight, reconstruct your experience, and

facilitate positive action in your life. If you're looking for more than "Dear Diary" writing, you're going to like this book.

* **You need to write about both the facts and your feelings about the facts.** In studies on therapeutic writing, those who wrote about superficial topics or just the facts of the crisis, without addressing their feelings, did not experience health benefits.

* **Timing might matter.** A few studies have found that people who were required to write about a traumatic event immediately after it occurred actually felt worse after expressive writing, possibly because they are not yet ready to face it[24]. My advice is to try it. See if it helps. If you find you're not ready, put this book down and wait a week or two. Then try it again.

* **Monitor yourself and do what makes sense for you.** Dr. Pennebaker has something called the flip out rule (which, when I did my training with him, I swear I heard him call the "freak out rule," so that's what I've been using with my clients ever since!). Basically, the advice was that only we know if we're about to flip out from our writing, and if we're getting close to that point, we should stop and do something else to calm ourselves down.

* **Therapy is helpful** (and yes, I'm biased, but it's true!). This book will provide you with therapeutic principles, wisdom, and tools that are similar to those you would receive in psychotherapy. That being said, the writing you do will bring up material that may be quite helpful to discuss in therapy. I highly encourage you to work with a mental health professional if you want to dive deeper into the material that comes up.

WRITING PROMPTS

Try your hand at responding to the writing prompts below. You can respond to some or all of the prompts, and you can do so on a single day or spread out your writing over several days this week.

My Journal

Take five or ten minutes and write about how you want to use this book and its writing exercises. When will be the best time for you to do your writing? In the morning, in the afternoon, before bed? How can you reduce other distractions in your environment so that you can have fifteen to twenty minutes at a time for uninterrupted writing? Which do you prefer, writing longhand or typing? How will you know if writing is helping? At what point would you seek the help of a mental health professional?

A Perspective Change

Write about a time in your life when your perspective about something changed. Choose a time when your eyes were opened to a new way of looking at and understanding something about yourself, your relationships, your health, your future, and/or your life in general.

What was this change in perspective? What impact has this change in perspective had on you and your life?

Are You a Night Bloomer?

- Are you in the dark? What happened to put you in this situation?

- How did you feel about life before your current situation?

- Do you feel you need a perspective change? Are you asking "why?" or "why me?" Or are you asking "what now?" What might happen if you started asking "what now?"

- In what ways do you relate to the stories about Night Bloomers in this chapter?

- Would you like to be a Night Bloomer? Why or why not?

Searching for Pearls

The burden of suffering seems to be a tombstone hung around our necks. Yet in reality, it is simply the weight necessary to hold the diver down while he is searching for pearls.

—Julius Richter

- What do you think about this perspective on pain and suffering?

- What does this perspective bring up for you?

- Is this your current perspective on suffering? If not, would you like it to become your perspective? What would it take to make this your perspective on your suffering?

WRITING TIPS FOR NIGHT BLOOMERS

Here are some writing tips to keep in mind as you create your *Night Blooming Journal*:

- Date your entries. It's nice to look back and see how far you've come.

- Grammar and spelling do not matter. These exercises are not designed to improve your technical writing skills; they're designed for healing and transformation.

- There is no right or wrong way to write. So, try not to judge, censor, or correct your journaling.

- Be as honest as possible. You only cheat yourself if you hold back the full truth.

- Write quickly and keep your hand moving. Write through the negative thoughts and emotions that come up.

- Write deeply. What you get out of writing will depend on how much you put into it.

- Keep your journal private and write for your eyes only. This will help you be as honest as possible.

- When you feel stuck, remember to tell your story just one word at a time.

- We're going to do more than just write about your pain. A lot more. Allow yourself to play and have fun.

CHAPTER 1

SETTING AN INTENTION TO BLOOM

Change is inevitable. Growth is intentional.
—GLENDA CLOUD

The first principle of blooming in the dark is *Setting an Intention to Bloom*. Before we get to why this is important and how one goes about setting an intention to bloom, let's get even more clear about what blooming in the dark is all about.

Resilience. It's a popular word these days. Maybe when you think of blooming in the dark, you think of resilience. It's a similar concept, but not quite the same. There are many different ways of defining resilience. The American Psychological Association defines resilience as "the process of adapting well in the face of adversity, trauma, tragedy, threats, or significant sources of stress. It means 'bouncing back' from difficult experiences"[25]. Similarly, the Department of Homeland Security[26] defines resilience as "the ability to resist, absorb, recover from, or successfully adapt to adversity or a change in conditions." A meme on the internet said resilience is "the courage to come back"[27]. I like that definition the best.

Adapting or "coming back" can mean any number of things. It might mean getting back in the driver's seat after experiencing a car accident. Or, interviewing for another job after being rejected by the

1

last ten companies with whom you've interviewed. Or, falling in love again after you have been betrayed. To me, resilience is about not letting an adversity define you or your dreams.

Blooming in the Dark Is More than Being Resilient

Blooming in the dark includes the idea of resilience, but it's about even more than that. When you bloom in the dark, you don't just bounce back from a trauma or adapt to adversity—you become *more* as a result of that trauma or adversity. Let me use an example of a coil spring to help explain what I mean. When a spring gets pushed down, and then the pressure is released, what does it do? Your first answer might be, "It springs back into the shape it was before." That picture or answer would be the essence of resilience. Coming back to one's original state.

But there's more to the picture than that. When you push down on a spring that is, for instance, resting on a table, you have to use a degree of force. It takes some energy to collapse those rings onto one another, and that energy has to go somewhere. When you release your finger, the energy inside the spring is released, and with a boing! the spring expands upward. If you watch carefully, you'll see that the spring stretches out farther and becomes longer than it had been originally, before it was collapsed upon itself. Already the spring is becoming more as a result of having been under pressure.

The "moreness" doesn't stop there. When you release the pressure of your finger from the spring, it doesn't just bounce back to its original state. The spring actually lifts off the table it was resting on and is propelled upward and forward. The larger the spring and the greater the pressure put on it, the farther it will go. The spring will become more, *permanently more,* as a result of having been under pressure.

When we choose to bloom in the dark, we are allowing the pressure exerted upon our lives to infuse us with the energy we need to propel forward in our lives. We don't become more despite the pressure; we become more as a result of the pressure. A spring can't "spring" unless it collapses and momentarily doesn't look like a spring at all. As Night Bloomers, we can't "spring" forward into a more incredible version of ourselves without something collapsing in our lives either. Like the spring, when that trial or trauma comes, for a while we might not resemble the people we used to be. It looks and often feels like we're smaller, weaker, and less than our previous selves.

But despite how it looks and feels, that's not the truth of the situation. The truth is that while we're in that down position, looking and feeling like less than we were, we are absorbing the energy we need to become even more glorious than we were before that trial came. We're absorbing the nutrients to grow.

Do you see it? The weight of that pain has not been placed on you to destroy you. No, that weighty pain is there to give you what you need to grow and bloom.

People Who Bloom in the Dark Become More than They Were

Let's return to the examples we used earlier to help define resilience: the driver driving again, the job seeker seeking again, the lover loving again. Now let's take it a step further and see what it would look like if these people bloomed in the dark, allowing their adversity to propel them forward in life. The woman didn't just drive her car again after the accident, she also became a more patient driver and a more patient person in general. Her character permanently changed, and this change significantly improved her relationship with her husband, children, and friends.

The man didn't just continue to interview for jobs after experiencing a series of rejections. He took the time to do some difficult soul-searching with the help of a therapist and realized that deep down he didn't believe he was worth hiring. He expected rejection, not just from potential employers, but from everyone in life. He worked through this negative self-belief and not only did he interview well and get the job, but he also started enjoying life in a brand new way. His whole outlook was more positive and engaging.

The woman who had been betrayed didn't just fall in love again; this time she loved with her whole being. She fully engaged in her next relationship and experienced a level of intimacy that she didn't even know existed. This second relationship was far more fulfilling than her first one. Through her experience of loss, she learned how to really love a man and how to receive his love.

In these examples, the individuals weren't just resilient, meaning they didn't just refuse to let an adversity define them or their dreams. These individuals bloomed in the dark. They allowed the force that collapsed something in their lives to be the very energy that caused them to become a better version of themselves.

You Must Get Your Hopes Up

How many times have you been told (or even said it yourself), "Don't get your hopes up!" We've been conditioned to think that it will hurt more if we get our hopes up and then they don't come true. We rationalize that if we set our sights lower, we won't be as disappointed. In the medical field, I've heard my colleagues say things like, "I didn't want to give my patient false hope, so I made sure they knew the chances were slim for … [a cure, a positive response to a new treatment, a speedy recovery, and so on]."

My heart always sinks when I hear things like this. Hope is a powerful force and critical ingredient for healing and transformation. We must get our hopes up if we want to bloom in the dark. In fact, it's so important that we'll return to the idea of feeding our hope in a few chapters.

For now, try thinking about getting your hopes up as setting an intention or an expectation for a future outcome. Why is this important? Because, in general, we get what we expect. I don't mean this in the way of the Law of Attraction (although I do think there's something to this idea energetically that we don't fully understand). In the world of psychology, this principle is called the self-fulfilling prophecy. When we expect something, we act in ways that line up with our expectation. These actions help to bring about the thing we expect. For example, if we expect to have a fun evening with friends, we likely arrive in good spirits and eagerly engage in the conversation. Our positive attitude and engagement is felt by our friends and is reciprocated. We feel encouraged and pleased that we are being responded to well and this inspires more positive feelings and actions. Eventually, by the end of the night, we have created a fun evening for ourselves.

Conversely, if we expect to be miserable, we will likely arrive with a poor attitude and either withdraw from the conversation or contribute in negative and critical ways. This will not be received well by the people we are with, who will send subtle or not-so-subtle messages of their disappointment or disapproval. These messages will further confirm our expectation that this was going to be a miserable evening, and we will end the night having experienced exactly what we expected to experience.

Our Beliefs Are Powerful

The placebo effect is another example of the power of hope or expectations. A placebo is an inert substance that doesn't have any healing properties in and of itself. However, people can experience benefits from an inactive substance, such as a sugar pill, just by *expecting* that it will help. When this happens, it's called the placebo effect. Researchers at Harvard Medical School found that, remarkably, our bodies can adjust our experience of pain relief from a medication just by altering the information we're given and (presumably*) the expectations we have as a result of this information[28].

Throughout the study, each patient received true, false, or uncertain information about the pill they were taking to help reduce their migraine

---

* The researchers suspect the effect was due to a change in participants' expectations, but since they did not specifically measure expectation change, they were hesitant to use this word.

pain. Sometimes they were given pain medication and were told they were taking pain medication (true condition), and sometimes they were given a placebo pill and were told it was a placebo pill, meaning it was inert (i.e., a sugar pill) and would not have an effect on their pain (also true condition). In the false condition, they were either given the real medication and told it was a placebo (to lower expectations) or given the placebo and told it was the medication (to raise expectations). Finally, in the uncertain condition, they were given a pill and told it could be either a placebo or the medication.

Here's what happened. People who received the pain medication experienced a greater reduction in pain than those who received the placebo pill. And, those who received the placebo pill did better than no treatment. These two findings were expected (no pun intended!). Now here's where it gets interesting, where we start to see the power of information and expectancies. People who were given the migraine medication but were told it was a placebo pill experienced less pain relief than when they were told they were getting the medication (false condition to lower expectation). In other words, the pain medicine was less effective when people didn't believe it was medicine.

Furthermore, people who received the placebo pill and were told it was medicine (false condition to raise expectation) experienced more relief from their pain than if they were told they got the placebo pill. In fact, they experienced the same amount of relief as those who received the medicine, but were told it was a sugar pill! In other words, the placebo was more effective when participants believed they were actually getting the medicine.

These results, and those from hundreds of other similar studies, demonstrate that what we expect impacts us, and it does so at the very neuro-cellular level. The effects of pain medication can be blocked by what we believe. Not only that, but we can also create pain relief in our body just by believing we are doing something that is going to reduce pain. I believe this pain relief isn't just applicable to physical pain; our beliefs impact our experience of emotional pain, too. The bottom line of the research on the placebo effect and self-fulfilling prophecies is that we get what we expect. And given that, it is so important that we be intentional about what we expect and use this power for our good.

Your Expectation Is Your Choice: Choose Wisely

But when we've been pummeled by life, it can be very hard to expect things to get better, especially when the pummeling just seems to keep on coming. It can also feel scary to expect things to get better, because what if they don't? Then what? It can feel unbearable to think of having to go through more pain and disappointment. However, what I've noticed in my own life and in the lives of my clients is that it's far better to hope for change and not see it than it is to sink in the pit of hopelessness and despair and resignation.

You see, here's the real kicker: You are never expectation free. You're always expecting something. You're either expecting nothing to change, for things to get worse, or for things to get better. Given what we know about the self-fulfilling prophecy and placebos, it's clear that we can change our reality with our beliefs. Remember in the Introduction we learned about how our perception *is* our reality? This is where the rubber hits the road. Where you get to make a choice. Where you get to set an intention. Up-level your expectations. Set yourself up to bloom in the dark.

You didn't have a choice about going through the suffering you're experiencing right now. But you do have a choice about how you want to respond to it and who you want to become as a result of it. That's what I mean by setting an intention to bloom. Blooming or transformation isn't an automatic process; it's one that requires clarity, intention, determination, and persistence.

Indeed, very few of the things we want to accomplish in life happen automatically. For most everything, we have to set a clear intention (i.e., set our belief and expectation for something), and for most everything, we have to exert some effort and persist in that expectation and effort until we realize our goal. It all begins with the intention we set. The research is clear: What we set our mind on—our intention—affects how things turn out.

Setting an intention: That's the first step of blooming in the dark.

Your Turn

Below are some writing prompts designed to help you set your intention for blooming. You'll engage in "possibility thinking," where you take the limits off of your current level of thinking and dream about how you'd like your situation and life to turn out. This type of thinking helps you to move beyond your current emotional state and challenging life situation. Then you'll get specific about what type of person you want to become, what character traits you want to develop, and what new focus you want for your life.

As you begin to set specific intentions for this time in your life, you'll start to notice a greater sense of control and agency despite being in the middle of difficult and uncertain circumstances. Although what we're doing is essentially setting goals for ourselves, it's different than making New Year's resolutions, which is important because hardly any of us keep those! This intention-setting work is deeper; it's soul work. We're creating a lifeline to your future self, shifting your perspective about what this time of suffering is all about, and creating new meaning and purpose for it. You're setting yourself up to be more than you could have been had this pain not happened. As you write, dream big and dig deep!

WRITING PROMPTS

Expectations and Harvests

- What are you expecting during this dark season? For yourself, for others, for how it all turns out?

- What harvest do you *really* want?

- What expectation or intention would lead to the harvest you desire?

Everything Is Possible

Let's play for a few minutes. Imagine that you were visited by an all-powerful and loving being who silently presented you with a beautiful gift wrapped in gold foil, just big enough to fit in the palm of your hand. The being disappears as soon as it hands you the gift. Warm light seems to emanate from the small package. You open the gift carefully and inside, wrapped in layers of golden tissue paper, is a little slip of paper. On the slip of paper written in gold ink is the following message: "From now on, there are no more limitations in your life. Everything is possible for you."

What would this message mean for you? What would you allow yourself to believe, to expect, to hope for that you haven't been allowing yourself? What limitations would end? What is the first thing you would do? What's the second thing?

Setting Your Intention to Bloom

While you are still in the germinating seed state, this is the perfect time to set your focus and intention to be in full bloom. In order to set the intention to bloom, you need to first define what blooming in the dark specifically means to you. Take a good twenty minutes to respond to the following prompts:

- In a few sentences, describe your darkness (i.e., your pain, suffering, loss).

- What does blooming in the dark mean to you?

- Who do you want to be at the end of all this?

- If you were to become that fully bloomed person, what would that look like? In other words, how would you or I know that you had bloomed in the dark?

- If we thought of the petals of your bloom as character traits, what would your petals be?

- When I was in the dark, I used to say, "I didn't ask for this hell, but you better believe that if I have to go through it, I'm going to come out better on the other side." What's your intention statement?

Your Blooming Word

For the last few years, instead of making New Year's resolutions, I have chosen a word for the year. The word represents my theme for the year, who I want to be, what I want to attract into my life, what I want my life to be about for the next 365 days. It's been remarkably effective and a lot of fun. It's a simple way to set an intention for the year. My goals then revolve around achieving this word. One year, my word was Joy, and I focused my daily efforts on creating and cultivating joy in my life. It was one of the most joyful years I've ever had.

Instead of choosing a word for the year, I invite you to choose a word for your blooming process. If you were to choose <u>one word</u> to represent what you want your blooming process to be all about, what word would you choose? Try brainstorming a long list of words and then choose the one that resonates best.

To help you choose your word, consider these questions:

- Who do you want to be when this is all over?

- What do you want to attract in your life?

- What do you want to embody during this time?

- What would be the greatest treasure or ideal harvest as a result of this time in the dark?

- What word inspires you?

Once you've chosen your blooming word, answer the following questions.

- If you were to live this word daily, how would your life be different one year from now?

- What are three habits that will help you to live out this word?

My Blooming Home Run Story

In this final prompt, write the story you want to be able to tell about yourself and your life once this dark season is over. In other words, write your *home run blooming year.*

Date your page one year from now. Now, describe in detail what happened, how you feel, what you accomplished, what you manifested, what types of thoughts you had, what type of person you have become, and so on. Write your best-case scenario year for blooming—write BIG! Be sure to write in the Present Tense (e.g., I have, I am, I feel, and so on).

BLOOMING CHECK-IN

1. What came up for you as you completed your writing prompts in this chapter? You might have noticed certain thoughts, emotions, themes, insights, or even resistance and doubt. Did anything surprise you?

2. In what ways did you grow this week, even just a little bit? Did you make any changes? What are you proud of?

3. How will you continue to apply this blooming principle in your life?

BLOOMING TIP

Congratulations on working your way through the first principle of blooming in the dark! Like our beliefs, our written words (which are just our beliefs and intentions translated onto the page) have creative power. To keep yourself moving in the direction of your intentions, it's important to continually remind yourself of your intentions. Take a moment now to think about the best way to do this for yourself. For example, you might read over your journal entries from this chapter once a week. Or you might write a blooming intention note to yourself and post it on your bathroom mirror or put it in your wallet where you'll see it every day.

If you're finding it hard to believe this new way of thinking about your pain and suffering, that's okay. For some of us, the perspective shift comes quickly; for others, we need more time to marinate in it and to make it our own. If you're finding yourself struggling with the idea of you blooming, try setting a timer for ten minutes. During those ten minutes, allow yourself to suspend your current reality and let your mind play with these ideas. Think about it like dipping one toe at a time into this new perspective. You don't need to be fully immersed yet. The important part is that you start dipping in and allowing your mind the opportunity to think about your situation from another perspective. We can't experience something until we've brought it into our realm of possibilities, and we do this by allowing ourselves to first believe that something is possible. After the ten minutes is up, you can go back to your former perspective. Every day, you might set the timer for a little longer, write a little more and a little deeper, and allow yourself to play with your blooming possibilities.

Creating a blooming vision and intention for yourself not only begins to build your hope, but it also provides an important container for the grief work that comes next.

~~

Night Bloomer: Darcy

When she was twenty years old, in her first year of college, Darcy fell head over heels for John, a senior who lived on the dorm floor above hers. Enjoying her new independence, Darcy found herself spending more and more time drinking with John and his friends. They introduced her to marijuana and soon she was drinking and smoking weed several nights a week. Many times she would black out from drinking too much. She had twinges of feeling like she was getting off track in life, but the excitement of living with fewer rules and dating an older man overshadowed what felt like minor concerns.

Then she started noticing unexplained bruises and scratches. She chalked it up to being clumsy when she was drunk. That is until one night—her twenty-first birthday—after having a celebratory drink with John at a bar, she woke up in his bed with him on top of her. She remembers feeling like she was drugged, and couldn't understand why she felt like this after having consumed only one drink. She lost consciousness and several hours later woke once again to John forcing himself inside her. This happened three times that night. Finally, she regained consciousness and, finding John asleep beside her, she texted her best friend to pick her up and quietly left.

She never reported the rape to the police, nor did she see John again. But the memory of him drugging and then raping her replayed in her mind like a nightmare on endless repeat. She was tormented by the fact that this may not have been the only time he had done that to her. She came to see me at the end of the semester. She was depressed, anxious, traumatized, and having frequent panic attacks. She was also cutting herself and drinking and using marijuana to cope with her emotional pain. She feared she'd never feel good again. The world was no longer a safe place, and although she longed for love and a romantic relationship, she was paralyzed with fear whenever she thought about dating again.

Darcy worked hard in therapy. We began by establishing a sense of safety in her environment and in her body, and then we processed the trauma and its aftereffects. After discussing the idea of blooming in the dark, she began a deep reflection on who she wanted to be and how she wanted to live her life going forward. Then she began the hard work of turning her blooming intentions into reality. She joined AA and stopped drinking, using marijuana, and cutting. She removed herself from her friend group, so as not to be tempted to engage in these destructive behaviors. She realized that she had chosen a major that didn't suit her, and so she courageously dropped out of the computer science program and enrolled in a creative writing program. She joined a poetry group and developed a new set of friends, including good guy friends. She got reconnected to her spirituality and her calling to be a healer in the world.

And she started writing. And writing. Besides blogging and journaling, over several months she wrote fifty-nine poems about the trauma, her brokenness and pain, and her path to healing and resilience. Through her beautiful and sometimes heart-wrenching poems, she narrated how she eventually found meaning in the devastation and darkness: "I found the gift in the darkness," she said, "and that gift was me." Indeed, the woman who emerged after the trauma was an even more beautiful and empowered version of the woman she was before going through this dark and painful time. Recently, she published her collection of poetry, dedicating it to anyone who has ever felt alone, broken, violated, or abused, to bring them comfort and hope in their healing process.

CHAPTER 2

GRIEVING BEFORE GROWING

Sorrows come to stretch out spaces in the heart for joy.
—L. B. COWMAN

In the last chapter, we set our intention for who we want to be at the end of the blooming process. This forward-looking step usually makes us feel hopeful and ready to get on with the good stuff. So I almost hate to say it, but just because we've got a vision of our future self, it doesn't mean that we're ready to bloom just yet. The next principle of blooming in the dark is a difficult one, but it is absolutely critical: *we must grieve our loss and feel our pain before we can grow.* Or put another way, we must mourn before we can adorn.

I know after hearing that, you might be tempted to stop reading and flip to the next chapter. But as hard as it may be, and as slowly as you may need to proceed through this material, please do not skip this chapter. Come back to the writing exercises later if you're not ready now, but please don't cheat yourself by thinking this step isn't for you.

Just like a seed must crack open before it can produce new life, so too must we acknowledge our grief and pain around our loss or life upheaval before we can experience healing and growth. Unfortunately, there is no shortcut to grief. Trust me, I've tried my best to find one for both myself and my clients. I've come to see what many before me have counseled: It's not until we let ourselves acknowledge and feel our grief that we are able to move through it.

The Hurting Time

In the novel *The Little Paris Bookshop* by Nina George, one of the characters gives some wise advice about grief to her friend, Jean Perdu, the main character. For years, Jean has been doing his best to run from his grief and anger over losing the love of his life. His grief is compounded by the guilt he feels about not seeing his love before she died. His friend says:

> *"Do you know that there's a halfway world between each ending and each new beginning? It's called the hurting time, Jean Perdu. It's a bog; it's where your dreams and worries and forgotten plans gather. Your steps are heavier during that time. Don't underestimate the transition, Jeanno, between farewell and new departure. Give yourself the time you need. Some thresholds are too wide to be taken in one stride."*

Grief is indeed a "hurting time," and as the name suggests, it requires time to move through, sometimes a lot of time. I would add to this advice that it matters what we do during this hurting time. Jean Perdu lost his love twenty years prior; he had two decades with his grief. Clearly, time hadn't healed his pain. But when Jean dedicated his attention to his grief, allowed himself to feel it, wrote and talked about it, and engaged in activities that were meaningful and healing for him, he was finally able to move through his grief and begin again. Jean called it "learning how to breathe under water." It all began when he gave grief his attention.

Emotional Pain Needs Our Attention Just Like Physical Pain

Think about the last time you got hurt physically. Maybe you cut yourself with a paring knife while chopping vegetables or with the razor when you were shaving. Or maybe you slammed the door on your finger or fell down the steps and twisted your ankle. What was the first thing you did? You stopped whatever you were doing and gave all your attention to the part of your body that was hurting, right? You did that because physical pain is designed to be a signal to stop and look. It's there to protect us. If we touch a hot stove and our finger throbs with searing pain, we stop everything we're doing, pay attention to what just happened, and remove our finger as quickly as possible from the burner. If we didn't, we'd lose our finger or worse. We might then put our finger under cold water or on ice or even see a doctor if the burns are severe. The point is we pay attention to the pain until we have done everything we can to set our finger up to heal.

Emotional pain works in the same way. It is a signal to stop and look. Yet, most of us don't give emotional pain the same level of importance and attention as we do physical pain. And that's unfortunate because without attending to our emotional pain, we can't set ourselves up to best heal. For many of us, emotional pain and suffering is far more difficult to handle than is physical pain. When I was going through the early days of my divorce, my friend Sarah said one of the most validating things. She said, "If anyone could see your heart right now, they'd admit you to the hospital's trauma unit. But no one can see it, so they think after a few weeks you should be fine. But your heart isn't fine. It's going to need a lot of attention and healing." The same could probably be said of you right now. Emotional pain must be attended to. I don't think it's too dramatic to say that your survival depends on it.

One of the reasons I chose writing as an avenue to facilitate the blooming process is because writing is an excellent way for us to stop and pay attention to our pain. We need to acknowledge our emotional pain before we can release it. When we take the time to write about our experience with suffering, we are acknowledging it with the intention of releasing it. Or to use the physical pain metaphor, writing is a way for us to attend to the wound, wash out the debris, apply healing ointment, and bandage it to promote a speedy and full recovery.

Grief as a Guest

Grief often comes with company. When grief "walked in my front door" and seemed ready to make a permanent home within me, close on its heels were sadness, despair, fear, and overwhelm. In the early days of my separation, I would spend hours on the floor in a fetal position making noises that I had never heard myself make before. I thought my soul was dying. It was frightening. Yet, at the same time, there was something healing about giving voice to my sadness, both on the floor and in my journal, especially when I had to spend most of my working day trying desperately to hold it together.

Maybe you are experiencing similar emotions to those I described above. Grief can also come with feelings of hopelessness, helplessness, anxiety, panic, resentment, irritability, disbelief, confusion, and numbness. It can feel like an emotional invasion, and you might wonder if you'll ever feel like yourself again. I found the poem "The Guest House" by Rumi, a Sufi poet, to be incredibly helpful in my times of emotional turmoil. In this poem, Rumi calls being human "a guest house" and says that every day we have emotional visitors (Did you hear that? Visitors! That means they aren't staying forever). He encourages us to "welcome and entertain them all." That was certainly not my first reaction when grief and his buddies forced themselves into my life. I wanted to kick every last emotion to the curb as quickly as possible.

But listen to why he tells us to welcome and even be grateful for these emotions as we would invited and honored house guests: "because each has been sent as a guide from beyond." Rumi is telling us that the sorrows and depression and dark thoughts are not here to destroy us, even though that's often how it feels when we experience them day after day. Indeed, the longer we feel them, the more they seem like maniacal house guests here to ruin our lives. Instead, Rumi suggests that these emotional guests are personal guides, and if we will welcome whatever emotions are showing up, we can receive their messages. To me, the most hopeful line in the poem is the one in which he says that even the most violent and difficult-to-bear emotions "may be clearing you out for some new delight." That puts a new spin on grief, doesn't it?

I am not suggesting we want to wallow in our grief. To the contrary, grief researchers assert it is important that we move back and forth, in and out of our grief processing[29]. We need times of focusing on our grief, as well as times of focusing on other things in our lives, even if that means using denial, avoidance, or distraction for a short period of time to give ourselves that relief and distance. What I am suggesting is that we don't need to fear our grief. In fact, if we can find a way to welcome it in for a time, we might just learn a thing or two and find that it hasn't come to make a permanent home in us, but rather to deliver a message and prepare us for something new, even a new delight.

It Isn't Just One Loss

Lest you are once again tempted to skip ahead thinking this chapter isn't relevant for you, it's important to know that acknowledging grief isn't just for people who have gone through a divorce or experienced the death of a loved one. We experience all kinds of losses and adversities in life, and many of these result in feelings of grief, if not many of the other emotions described above, too. On top of that, not only do we grieve the primary thing we lost—such as a loved one or a pet or a relationship or our health—we also mourn the other things we lost along with it. For example, when we lose a spouse, many of us also experience a loss of emotional support, a loss of parenting help, a financial loss, a loss of our identity as a wife or a husband, and social losses, such as no longer feeling comfortable attending couples' events as a single person.

Loss often also requires that we learn new skills and take on new responsibilities, which can feel stressful or overwhelming when we're grieving. Before my husband left, I had no idea how much went into taking care of a house. After he left, I had to figure out how to deal with the many details involved in home ownership. In the early days, it all seemed overwhelming and unfair. Little by little, as I mastered a task or fixed something that was broken, I noticed my confidence was building. I still can't say I enjoy the "joys" of home ownership, but I am a stronger, more capable woman as a result of taking on these new roles and responsibilities. It has given me a greater sense of independence and competence, for which I am grateful.

You, too, are likely dealing with more than one loss right now, losses as a result of your primary loss. Take time to acknowledge these additional losses. They contribute to the grief and other emotions you are feeling right now.

The Goal of Grieving Is Not Closure

To add insult to injury, when we are grieving, we are more likely to experience mental and physical health problems. Our defenses are down. We are worn out, past worn out, and this makes us vulnerable at every level. This is one of the reasons it is critical that we don't deny our grief and, at the same time, critical that we don't spend the rest of our lives mired in our grief. Like a tunnel, we need to move through it. And like a tunnel, I'm not sure we ever achieve "closure," whatever that means. When you lose something or someone you love, that loss never ends, just like the love you have for that person or thing doesn't end. Indeed, bereavement theorists have recognized the limitations of Kübler-Ross's popularized Stages of Grief theory. Very few of us move through linear stages of grief. Instead, grief experts recognize the importance of going through dynamic and flexible grief processes, including reconstructing a sense of meaning and recreating a relationship with the person or thing we lost[30].

For example, rather than trying to find "closure," we are now encouraged to find ways to have a continuing bond with the person or thing we lost[31]. Just because they are no longer physically present does not mean the bond or relationship has to end. Many of my grieving clients have reported profound relief and comfort when they found other ways to create and enjoy the bond they have with their loved one. Many still talk to their loved one. Others write letters. Some sit in the garden and commune with their loved one without words being spoken. What matters is that the bond is continued in a way that is meaningful to you.

When to Seek Help

Grief can make you feel like you are going crazy. Like you are out of control. I can remember standing in line at the grocery store and suddenly bursting into tears—more than once. Sometimes it was because something reminded me of my husband, other times it was because someone was randomly kind to me. Sometimes I had no idea why I was suddenly weeping. The whole experience felt very disconcerting, particularly because I tend to like to feel in control of my life, particularly of my emotional self in public! I learned, as you may have already too, that grief is like a wave. It can come suddenly and without warning, threatening to overwhelm and destroy. But like any wave, at some point it peaks and then it falls. Your job is to ride the waves. I promise as time goes by the emotional sea gets calmer and the waves come in less often. Although they may never completely cease, the intensity of the waves does decrease, as your ability to manage them as they come in increases.

We all grieve differently, and we grieve for different amounts of time. Some people feel like they need to apologize for their grief. Clients have said, "I'm so sorry, I shouldn't be crying like this over the loss of my dog. It could have been my child. I feel ridiculous grieving like this." To that I say, you never need to apologize for your grief. You're grieving because you loved something. Love is love and grief is grief. Take however much time you need to feel your feelings and mourn your loss. Grief is a normal part of life, as much as I wish that were not the case.

That said, if your grief has been persistent and endless, going on for a very long time with no relief or lessening, or perhaps even getting worse; you can't focus on anything but the person or thing you lost; and you experience intense emotional pain and are unable to experience any positive emotion, please talk to a mental health professional. There is a type of bereavement reaction recognized by the medical and mental health community as requiring professional help. Among other factors, sustaining multiple losses in quick succession without adequate time to heal in between can be one factor that sets some people up to experience this type of prolonged grief. A trained professional can help you determine if you fit into this category and provide you with the right treatment, so that you can finally heal.

Or if you're feeling down or depressed most of the day nearly every day or you've lost all interest in things you used to enjoy and this has lasted for more than a few weeks, please reach out to your doctor or a mental health professional. Even if you're not in one of these extreme states described above, you may still find it helpful to speak with a therapist. I know I did. Find one that is both compassionate and easy to talk to and who is trained to help people deal with grief and/or bereavement, depending on your specific type of loss.

Your Turn

In the following writing prompts, you will have the opportunity to acknowledge your pain and give voice to your suffering and grief. Think of the prompts as healing tools for your "hurting time." As we discussed earlier, the research shows that those who have the best outcomes after writing are those who wrote about both the facts of the situation and their feelings about those facts—not just one or the other. The prompts are designed to help you do both. The prompts also draw upon narrative therapy and trauma-focused therapy, both of which help people heal by telling and retelling (and telling again) their story. This retelling process helps the story to become integrated into their entire life story, and it loses its emotional intensity as it does. So, if it feels like you're writing about the same thing a number of times but in slightly different ways, you are! Some of the prompts may resonate with you and your particular loss more than others. Feel free to focus on these prompts. You can also modify any of the prompts to make them more applicable to you.

Also, remember what the research has found: We need both time to acknowledge our grief and time away from our grief[32]. Both are important for our healing. So, please do engage in the writing exercises below and do so at your own pace. I've designed the prompts to help you acknowledge and process your grief. But don't pitch your tent on this chapter, so to speak. The rest of the chapters and their accompanying writing exercises have also been designed to help you to move through your grief and find new meaning, purpose, and healing. The writing exercises in this chapter are a start, but they're just the beginning. Research has shown that a significant contributor to moving through grief is reconstructing meaning[31]. Although in this chapter you will be giving voice to your grief, and in doing so you may even begin this meaning-making work, the rest of the blooming principles are specifically designed to help you create meaning and reconstruct your narrative around your loss and adversity. Take heart, dear friend, there is a lot more blooming—and hope—in front of you.

Tips for Writing about Grief

It's not easy to dive into your pain. Here are a few tips to help you through this process so that you don't find yourself buried in the expression of your grief, but rather find some relief as you release it onto the page.

* I encourage you to set a timer before you begin writing. That way you can lose yourself in your writing for a set amount of time, but not find yourself mired in it for hours.

* Be sure to complete the first two "Getting Started" prompts before digging into the prompts related to grief. I've designed these to help you gather emotional resources you might find helpful as you go through this process.

* Plan something enjoyable to do, preferably involving other people, after you are finished writing.

* This isn't supposed to be easy. Remember, the research has shown that some people experience an increase in emotional distress and negative mood after writing about difficult topics. This is to be expected. But it will get better.

* Remember the flip out/freak out rule: If you're about to do either of these things, stop writing, take some deep breaths, do something calming, and return to your writing when you're ready.

* You may want the support of family, friends, and/or a good therapist as you begin to acknowledge and release your grief.

* Try the pick-me-up prompt at the end of each of your writing sessions in this chapter, as a way to finish the day's writing and processing on a more positive note.

WRITING PROMPTS

Getting Started: What Helps You Cope?

Given that you'll be writing about some tough things in this chapter, let's start out by gathering your resources. I invite you to make a list of all the ways you can make yourself feel calmer when you start to feel overwhelmed with negative emotions or memories. In other words, what helps you cope? These can be big things and small things—anything that makes you feel more positive or more relaxed. These are things you can do during or after your writing on grief. It's important to let ourselves feel our grief, and it's also important to let ourselves have a break from the grief. The resources you identify will help you do just that.

Getting Started: My Peaceful Place

Take a moment to make yourself comfortable. Close your eyes, uncross your legs if you're sitting in a chair, do something comfortable with your hands, and take some deep breaths. Focus on your breath for a few moments, letting each inhalation and exhalation relax you even more. Now, imagine visiting a place that feels peaceful to you—perhaps somewhere you have been to before or have always wanted to go, or a place that only exists in your imagination. The important thing is that you feel peaceful in this place. When you have chosen your place, use your eyes like a movie camera and try to visualize it in as much detail as you can. What do you hear? What do you smell and taste? What textures do you feel? Notice how you feel emotionally in this peaceful place.

Now, open your eyes and write down a detailed description of your peaceful place. Give this place a name. If at any time you start to feel overwhelmed with negative thoughts or emotions while writing, you can stop and go to this peaceful place in your mind. This is a tool you can use whenever suffering and grief threaten to overwhelm you.

Classic Writing Prompt Instructions

The following is the classic writing prompt, developed by Dr. Pennebaker, that has been used in the expressive writing research. Although I would encourage you to try using this prompt to express the grief and loss that drew you to this book, studies have also shown that even when participants wrote about topics other than the prominent problem they had experienced, they still showed improvement.

For the next fifteen to twenty minutes, write about a traumatic or life-changing experience. In your writing, really let go and explore your very deepest emotions and thoughts. You might tie this trauma to your childhood and your relationships with others, including parents, lovers, friends, or relatives. You may also link this event to your past, your present, or your future, or to who you have been, who you would like to be, or who you are now.

Not everyone has had a single trauma, but all of us have had major conflicts or stressors—and you can write about these as well.

Try to use this same prompt to write for fifteen to twenty minutes each day for the next three days. You may write about the same general issues or experiences on all days or write about different topics each day.

Because It Mattered

> *"I said to someone I know, 'I don't know why this hurts so much.'*
> *And she said, 'it hurts because it mattered.' And that was a huge thing*
> *for me to realize. That there are things in life that hurt.*
> *And they hurt because they were important."*
>
> —John Green

What do you think the author means by "it hurts because it mattered"? Can you identify with this idea? What in your life has hurt because it mattered?

What Hurts the Most?

One of the questions I often ask my clients when they are in pain is, What hurts the most right now? This might change day by day, or it might remain the same. Sometimes this is the hardest thing to talk about, and that often makes it the most important thing to talk about. It's like when you go to see your doctor—she wants to know where the pain is, so that she can address the root cause of your ailment. Similarly, try to get to the root cause of your pain in your writing. If it applies to you, another similar question you might answer is, What do you miss the most about the person or thing you lost? Let yourself go to these dark places for a few minutes. Use your resources during or after your writing, if you need to.

What Else Have You Lost?

Make a list of the other things you have lost as a result of your primary loss. These might fall in the categories of identity, family, social, spiritual, physical, mental, financial, emotional and practical support, and so on. Also list the new roles and responsibilities you have had to take on as a result of your loss. Now read your list. Do you feel any more compassion for yourself for feeling the way you do?

Gaining Distance: Tell Your Story in the Third Person

Some research has shown that writing from a different point of view—the third-person perspective rather than the first-person perspective—can be helpful for people who experience high levels of intrusive thoughts (i.e., thoughts about their situation or suffering that won't seem to leave them alone and come up even when they don't want to be thinking about it). In one study, when people with high levels of intrusive thoughts wrote in the third person, they reported more short-term and long-term perceived benefits from writing, as well as better health[34]. This is likely because writing in the third-person perspective allowed them to gain some emotional and cognitive distance from their pain and difficult life situation.

Try writing about your time in the dark, or a piece of the adversity you have experienced, in the third-person perspective (i.e., using she/her or he/his) instead of the first-person (i.e., I, me, or mine). In other words, try writing your story as if it happened to someone else. Notice if this writing technique helps you gain some emotional distance from your suffering.

Here's an example of writing in the first person: "When I was told I had been fired today, I felt a complete paralysis. I was so numb I was speechless. I walked out of the building in a daze."

Here's an example of writing in the third person: "When she was told she had been fired today, she looked paralyzed. She didn't speak and when she left the building, she seemed dazed."

Dialogue with My Lost Loved One

The following prompt can be helpful for people who have lost a loved one due to death or divorce or another event that has severed relational ties. For this writing exercise, imagine you are having a dialogue with your lost loved one. What would you like to say to him or her? Write this down. Then write down what you think he or she would say back to you. You can construct this conversation like a dialogue you might see in a story, with you both taking turns talking back and forth. Or you might write a letter to your loved one and then write a letter back to yourself from the perspective of your loved one.

When you have finished writing your dialogue or letters, answer the following reflection questions:

- What came up for you as you engaged in this dialogue?

- What do you think about what your loved one said to you? Was this comforting? Did it provide you with any insights?

- How could you use this writing technique to continue the bond between you and your loved one?

The Guest House

If you haven't already done so, read Rumi's poem "The Guest House." The poem is easily accessed on the Internet. Then answer the following questions:

- What did you notice in your body as you read this poem?

- What thoughts did you have?

- Do you see your emotions, even the most violent and difficult ones, as guests? Do you treat them honorably? If not, why not?

- What do you think of the idea of your emotions "clearing you out for some new delight"?

- How does this idea change the way you see and engage with your grief?

Wrapping Up with a Few Questions about Grief

- What would it be like to trust your hurting time (e.g., trust that grief is not going to destroy you; trust that it's not always going to feel this intense; trust that grieving is a part of the blooming process)? What keeps you from trusting your hurting time?

- Given the traumatic or stressful event(s) you just wrote about, what do you need in order to move toward greater peace and healing in your life?

- Is there anything else you need to acknowledge? Anything you've been ignoring or afraid to acknowledge?

- Is there anything you need to explore in your writing? If so, either make a note about it so you can come back to it later, or take some time now to write about it.

A Pick-Me-Up

Writing about your pain and feeling your grief is emotionally hard work. If you need a little pick-me-up after you've done your writing for the day, here's a prompt that can help shift your emotional state.

Take five minutes and write about a time when you felt happy or at peace. Or the last time you laughed. Or a time when you felt loved. Where were you? Who were you with? What was the weather like? Was there a specific thing that evoked this happiness? If so, what was it? Write down as many details as you can about this happy or peaceful time. Try to recapture the feeling in your writing.

Or, if the above ideas bring up sadness for you because those memories are linked to your loss and current pain, you might write about something or someone who makes you smile, or someone who loves you (pets included!), or something you love, or something you're grateful for.

Let yourself marinate in these positive emotions for a few minutes.

BLOOMING CHECK-IN

1. What came up for you as you completed your writing prompts in this chapter? Was it easier or harder than you expected to write about and feel your grief?

2. In what ways did you grow this week, even just a little bit? What are you proud of?

3. How will you continue to apply this blooming principle in your life?

BLOOMING TIP

I know this wasn't an easy chapter, and I'm proud of you for making it through, or making it through as much as you can for right now. If you're feeling tired or blue or low on energy, that's normal. You've been doing some emotional heavy lifting!

As you are spending time processing your grief and suffering through writing, remember to take good care of yourself. Good self-care includes making sure you are getting enough sleep, eating a healthy diet, engaging in some form of exercise, spending time with people who care about you, nurturing your spirituality, working with a therapist, and participating in activities that nourish and rejuvenate you.

Grieving is a challenging, but critical, part of the blooming process. Some of you will need to spend a long time on this step (just like some physical wounds take longer to heal than others), and many of you will need to revisit this step throughout your process. It's important not to hurry through this step. I promise your future self will thank you for doing the hard work now.

CHAPTER 3

SUPPORTING YOUR BLOOM

There must be those among whom we can sit down and weep,
and still be counted as warriors.

—ADRIENNE RICH

Being in the dark is hard. Sometimes it feels easier to give up than to keep pressing on toward blooming. The truth is, it probably would be easier to give up, at least in the short term. As we discussed before, blooming requires intention, determination, perseverance, and patience. All of these things require energy, and when you're in pain, there barely feels like enough energy to make it through the basic necessities of a day, let alone energy left over for transformation. If we're honest, a good number of us have had at least a fleeting thought that it would be easier if it was all over. Not that we are contemplating ending our lives, although sadly some are in such anguish they see no way out other than suicide. My heart breaks for those individuals. I wish we could hook them up to a "hope IV" for a few hours to supercharge their ability to see their way through the dark. But the thought that things would be better if you didn't wake up in the morning is a pretty common one when your life falls apart.

This chapter is about helping to prevent you from sinking into that kind of despair (or helping you get out if you're there right now) and also to reach the blooming intention you have set for yourself. I've called this third blooming principle *Supporting Your Bloom*. In a nutshell, it means don't try to get through your darkness alone. We need to get and stay connected to others, especially during the difficult times in life.

Only the Strong and the Brave Ask for Help

There are a lot of reasons why we are reticent to reach out for help. When we're in pain, it's not uncommon to feel alone or actively withdraw from others, wonder if something is wrong with us, experience low energy, or feel anxious or afraid. It's also not uncommon to think that we don't need help, wish that we didn't, or try to prove that we don't. In the Western world we prize independence. Being able to do things on our own makes us feel strong and successful. Asking for help or the idea of being dependent on another is looked down upon as weak, as if the help seeker is lacking in confidence or competence or both. As a result, asking for help and support can come with a large serving of stigma and shame in our society.

I disagree with this negative perspective of asking for help. Perhaps it has something to do with me being in a helping profession and knowing how much courage it takes for people to admit they're struggling and need some assistance. Or perhaps it's because I know firsthand how crucial the support of others has been for me when I've been in the dark. In my opinion, asking for help is a brave act, one that requires a great deal of inner strength. The act of reaching out is a choice not to surrender to despair and hopelessness. And only a strong and courageous person can make that choice, even and especially when there are very few indications that change is up ahead. I admire a person who has the courage to say, I need some help. Or, I need some company. Or, I need a hug. A long one, please.

It's Time to Get Staked

Have you ever noticed that some plants are given more support as they are growing than are other plants? These supported plants often have wooden or metal stakes placed alongside them to which they are tied. Some are even placed inside of a large circular cage, such that they are fully encompassed by this supportive structure. As ironic as this may sound, given this book is based on a gardening metaphor, I do not have a green thumb, nor do I know a whole lot about gardening. So, I did some research on why some plants are supported like this.

Turns out that plants need support when they 1) are newly transplanted; 2) bear a lot of fruit, especially heavy fruit; 3) have large clusters of flowers; 4) are particularly tall; and/or 5) need protection from the elements, such as heavy rains and wind. Plants such as tomatoes, pole beans, cucumbers, squash, snapdragons, dahlias, and zinnias fit into one or more of these categories and need to be staked while they are still young and growing. I learned that once a stalk is bent or broken, getting the plant to stand up straight again can be very challenging. The purpose of staking a plant is to provide it with support, which prevents it from breaking as it grows and ensures it reaches its full potential. Staking, in other words, is an essential step for some plants to bloom.

You know what else needs to be "staked"? Night Bloomers. We're "newly transplanted" in that our worlds have been turned upside down and we've been planted in a new garden, often one we didn't ask for and don't particularly like. We've set our intention to bear a lot of fruit or blooms and to stand up tall and strong as a result of being in the dark. And we're facing what feels like more than our fair share of the "elements" or stressors during this time. In other words, as much as we might hate to admit it, we're vulnerable and we need extra support, so that we don't flop over or break under the weight of the suffering we're experiencing.

Assembling Your Stakes (aka Your Support Team)

By far, the best kind of "stake" or support for Night Bloomers is other people. The research is abundantly clear: Individuals who are supported by others are healthier, are happier, and live longer. They also are less likely to be negatively affected by stress[35]. Conversely, not only does isolation and loneliness set us up for depression and other health problems, but it also increases our likelihood of mortality by 26 percent[36]. In fact, some research has shown that isolation and loneliness is just as bad for us as smoking[37]! Interestingly, we don't even necessarily need to receive the support from others to benefit. Just thinking about the social support that we have available to us has a beneficial impact on our well-being[38].

That being said, it can feel incredibly lonely when you're suffering, even if you have a good support system. I remember during those first few months after my separation when I'd go out with friends, I'd still feel alone. Even when I was sitting right there in their presence. I knew they loved me and would do anything for me. They couldn't take away the pain, though, and they didn't understand how much it hurt. It's not their fault that they didn't understand. I didn't even know pain like that existed until I went through it myself, and I'm a clinical psychologist. How could they? But, it was important that I still spent time with them, and it's important you do, too, even if you feel alone at first.

One of the fears I hear a lot from my clients who are dealing with depression and grief is that of burdening or bringing others down with their sadness. "I don't like being around myself right now," they say, "how could anyone else want to be around me?" Yet, the research is clear that it is then that they most need to be surrounded by others. In order to alleviate some of this fear, I often suggest that they build themselves a team. In this way, no one person bears the whole weight of providing support.

In addition to me as their therapist, this might look like a few friends they can confide in deeply; other friends with whom they just spend time and have fun (rather than share about their emotional state); family members; other professional healers, such as an acupuncturist, massage therapist, energy healer, physical trainer, and so on; a support group; and a clergy member or spiritual director, if this fits within their belief system. I also encourage them to make at least one social contact a day that is not through text or social media. Although these methods of digital communication play a role in helping us to stay connected, there is nothing that compares to real-life interaction, and at the very least, a phone call.

When you are in the acute stage of loss or tragedy, your family and friends often rally around you. But over time, that support and contact start to decrease. That's natural, and there are all kinds of reasons why their contact or how often they ask about you or your situation diminishes besides them feeling burdened. Even if feeling burdened is the case for a few, that's ok. Remember, we're looking for a team, not just one individual. I've found that a lot of the time people don't realize that you still need or want to talk about how you are doing. They think that it's better to let you bring it up. So, if you still need support—and if you're in the dark, you still need support!—then sometimes it's on us to ask for it. The phone call, the cup of tea, the shoulder to cry on, the company on a lonely Friday night, the drive to the doctor's office, the help around the house, or the encouragement that it won't always feel so bad.

Another way you can build your support team is to form or join a "blooming group." This is a group for Night Bloomers that falls somewhere in between a book club and a support group. Unlike a regular book club, the purpose of a blooming group is not so much to discuss the book, the author, or the literary choices and devices. A blooming group also differs from a typical support group or grief group in that the focus is less on the darkness and more on the blooming. The purpose of the group is to advance the blooming process of each individual member. It does so by using the principles and writing prompts provided in *Night Bloomers*. Not only does a blooming group help you to assemble your own garden stakes, but it also provides you with the opportunity to be a support for others during their difficult time. I provide more information at the end of the book on how to start your own blooming group.

You Need People Who Will Tell You the Truth

In addition to providing us with emotional support or practical support, such as looking after our kids when we need to go to a doctor's appointment or the lawyer's office, there is another vital reason why we need to surround ourselves with loving and supportive people when we're in pain: We need people who will tell us the truth. When we're in the dark, we need truth like we need air to breathe and water to drink. We can go without a lot of things when we are in pain, but we cannot go long without the truth.

When you're going through loss or your life has been turned upside down, you will be bombarded with messages about who you are, what you're going through, and why you are experiencing this pain. You may find yourself questioning everything you once held true. Perhaps someone who was supposed to care about you says poisonous things about your character. Or perhaps someone tells you that you got cancer because you didn't think positively enough or are being punished for something you did wrong. Or that you lost your child because God wanted her back. Sometimes we even tear ourselves down with our own words.

If we listen to the wrong voices during this vulnerable time, just like plants that need to be staked and aren't, our fragile stems can break under the pressure, and it can be very difficult to recover from these injuries of untruth. We need the loving voices of the people who care about us to remind us who we really are, what our potential is, that we are loved, and that we have every reason to believe that we won't be in the dark forever. We also need people to tell us the truth when we're not doing our work in the darkness and instead are just wallowing in despair or self-pity.

Finally, not everyone who is in your garden (i.e., your social support team) is there for you to share the details of your suffering with. Some people are there to help you continue to live out your roles and responsibilities in life. Indeed, I think it's critical that we have people in our garden with whom we do not discuss our loss and grief. These might be people like your boss, some of your colleagues, your banker or dentist, your patients, and your employees. These people play an important role in our garden. They give us opportunities to reconnect to parts of ourselves that are not mired in grief. These people allow us to put on our professional clothes (literally and figuratively) and do something useful, even if it's not our best work right now. The gift they offer us is their confidence in us to do something other than grieve. For us to "carry on."

Your Turn

In the following journal prompts, you will have the opportunity to reflect on who is in your garden already and the roles that each of these people play. The research shows that just this act of reflecting on your current social support has benefits for your well-being. Then you'll write about what other support you need right now and ways to find that support. You'll come up with some concrete steps to increase your social support and to "stake" yourself to this support while you're making your way through the darkness.

WRITING PROMPTS

Taking Stock of Your Support Stakes

Take a few minutes and make a list of each person who is already in your garden (i.e., who is on your social support team—who provides you with emotional, practical, or truth-telling support, or the opportunity to "carry on" and fulfill your responsibilities in life, or another kind of support). Beside each name, write the kind of support this person provides and how this makes you feel.

Adding Helpful Stakes

Now think about what other kind of support you would benefit from during this time. Perhaps as you were taking stock, you noticed that you were missing or didn't have much of a certain type of support. Maybe you have a lot of informal, personal support, but not a lot of professional support, or vice versa. Write about what other kinds of support you would like.

Then, write about where you might find this kind of support. This might mean asking someone in your circle if he or she would be willing to provide this kind of support for you. Or it might mean looking up the names of local therapists or contacting someone at your place of worship who might offer you counsel.

Finally, write down two or three practical things you will do this week to add these stakes (i.e., team members) to your garden.

Removing Unhelpful Stakes

Is there anyone in your social support circle who brings you down? Who makes you feel worse about yourself or your situation? If so, perhaps it is time to remove these stakes from your garden. That doesn't necessarily mean you need to remove them from your life altogether, but if they are hindering your ability to heal and move forward, you may not want them in your inner support circle. Write about what comes up for you as you think about this idea.

When I'm Connected

Think about the last time you felt really connected or supported by someone. Describe that situation. Who provided the support, what kind of support was it, what was your reaction, and how did you feel?

My Quick-Fix Support Plan

Make a plan for the next time you are feeling lonely or sad. Our tendency is to isolate ourselves when we feel this way. Try doing the opposite next time. Write down who you can contact and what you can say when this happens. How do you think this will make you feel? Are you willing to be brave and try this? Why or why not?

Connecting to My Stakes This Week

Beside each day of the week, write the name of one person that you will reach out to and how you will reach out to them. Ideally, you would see the individual in person or call them on the phone (bonus points for video chats!). If you are unable to do this, then a text or email is okay, as long as that's not the norm. You'll feel more filled up inside if you have "real" person-to-person contact.

- Monday

- Tuesday

- Wednesday

- Thursday

- Friday

- Saturday

- Sunday

BLOOMING CHECK-IN

1. What came up for you as you completed your writing prompts in this chapter? Did you notice anything different from your writing in previous chapters?

2. In what ways did you grow this week, even just a little bit? Did you make any changes? What are you proud of?

3. How will you continue to apply this blooming principle in your life?

BLOOMING TIP

In this chapter, we've focused on reaching out and making contact with others as a way to support ourselves as we make our way through the dark. There is also some interesting research that suggests that providing support to others is also an effective way to boost our mood and well-being. I read a story on the Internet recently about an immigrant couple who helped a man on the side of the road with a flat tire. The man tried to give the couple money for helping him. The couple wouldn't take his money. The husband said, "Today you, tomorrow me."

And he's right. Quite simply, we need one another. I invite you to think about who is in your garden, centrally or peripherally, who might also be in need of support. Are there any small or big ways you might provide that person with some support? If you try this, I encourage you to write about your experience and the impact it has on your mood.

Night Bloomer: Renée

The following story about the power of Writing for Wellness is from one of my clients, who went through a long journey to heal and transform following a diagnosis of breast cancer. Renée offered to write this excerpt to inspire others with hope that they too can bloom in the dark, and to share how writing helped her find her treasures and transformation in the dark.

MY DARKNESS

After years of a mysterious, steady decline in my health, I was blindsided with an early-stage breast cancer diagnosis at age forty-two. Having endured and successfully navigated a devastating disability diagnosis in our only child two years earlier, my cancer diagnosis was not the worst news. Rather, it was part of a series of nightmarish events including my mother's diagnosis of multiple myeloma just one year prior to mine.

Instinctively, I was convinced that I had developed this condition for a reason, and that it was essential that I explore and come to understand why and how I fell so ill at this age. Although there was much work to be done between managing my health and my daughter's, I set about the business of healing, and what I would later call blooming in the dark.

I received the standard of care for my diagnosis, which involved surgery, radiation, and five years on a hormone blocker. Disenchanted and frightened by the adverse effects (real and prospective) of my conventional cancer care, I was also desperate to educate myself on other safe, evidence-based cancer therapies. Journaling or writing for wellness was one of the healing activities suggested to me. It, along with qigong and meditation, would ultimately prove to be one of my most important healing tools.

HOW I USED JOURNALING AS A TOOL

I enrolled in Dr. Pearce's *Writing for Wellness* four-week workshop and I learned the art and methodology of writing to heal, just as they are outlined in this book. I could tell that the instructions, suggestions, and prompts were working, and that this was a marked improvement over how I had been journaling. However, it would be years before I understood the extent to which writing in this way impacted my health. Over time I learned how to rewrite my life narrative. This ability to develop a new narrative disentangled from my family's long history of intergenerational trauma allowed me to shift from a place of inherent victimization to empowerment. However, I quickly learned that the benefits extended beyond this; that there were beautiful spiritual and energetic healing gifts, too.

JOURNALING HELPED ME TO HEAL AND BLOOM IN THE DARK

The sheer act of getting my thoughts and emotions out of my body and onto paper often provided an immediate release. Doing so could be grave at times, but I always felt lighter and fuller spiritually afterward. Seven years after my initial diagnosis, as I reviewed my journals recorded during the time of my treatment, I was stunned to see how the words that I had written and long since forgot had clearly set a foundation for healing. Even more stunning is how I healed according to what I had written. Somehow the therapeutic writing process had acted as a subconscious, spiritual flashlight, illuminating my path for healing during my darkest and most confusing times.

SHARING MY BLOOMING MESSAGE

After seven long, challenging years, I am thrilled to have recently been released from my oncologist's care with no evidence of disease. Not only have I made great progress with my physical health, my spiritual and mental health are also much improved. I am living a much more balanced and fulfilling life than I was prior to implementing these healing practices. I am also actively seeking ways to help others navigate the confusion and fear that often come with a cancer diagnosis and to find healing and transformation during their dark time. To this end, I am pursuing a path as a holistic cancer coach. My hope is that my story inspires others to experience the benefits of this transformative tool for blooming in the dark.

CHAPTER 4

BEING IN THE DARK

The quest for certainty blocks the search for meaning.
Uncertainty is the very condition to impel man to unfold his powers.

—Erich Fromm

One of the most difficult aspects of loss and life upheavals is the uncertainty of it all. Being in limbo is an uncomfortable state. Will I recover? Will I find a new job? Will we lose the house? Will my spouse come back? Will we ever have a child? Will I love again? Will I ever feel normal again? These kinds of questions can haunt us while we're in the dark. The uncertainty of our futures can become almost as painful as the loss we experienced.

We often set our hearts on a certain outcome—a restored relationship, a certain kind of lifestyle, or a cure for a disease, for example—yet because we are not guaranteed this outcome, focusing on it can cause us a lot of fear and distress. In other words, our attachment to a certain external outcome can cause us even more suffering. Even if we're able to let go of the desired outcome, we have trouble sitting in and with the uncertainty of it all. We think, if I just knew how it all worked out, I would be okay, I could get back to living.

The fourth blooming principle seems obvious, but it's not easy; that is, *blooming in the dark actually requires being in the dark.* Being in the dark in terms of how it all turns out. There are things we just do not and cannot know during this time. Fighting against this uncertainty causes us an additional layer of suffering on top of an already painful time. We need to learn how not to fight it.

New Life Requires Being in the Dark

We can view being in the dark either as an undesirable state that we rail against or as something that contributes to our growth, uncomfortable as it may be. Think about seeds. Where are they when they start to grow? Basking in the warmth of the sunlight? No, they are buried deep down in the cold, dark soil for a long time before we begin to see the effects of their arduous labor to get to the surface. What about babies, where are they when they start to grow? Held tight in the darkness of their mother's womb. Nature is clear: New life begins in the dark. And this darkness is a good thing. It provides the much-needed protection for this vulnerable new life to take hold and develop into something that can sustain being in the light.

Just because you are in the dark and you don't know how it all works out doesn't mean there isn't a glorious future ahead of you. A few years ago, a friend and I were driving from Las Vegas to the Grand Canyon, where we planned to spend a few days hiking. I had never been before and couldn't wait to see the majesty of the place for myself. It took us three, maybe four hours to drive there. The longer we drove, the more confused and dismayed I became. I was not expecting that the majority of the drive would be mile after mile of flat, barren landscape, with only a few dusty cactuses dotted here and there. After a few hours of this, I started to worry that perhaps we had taken a wrong turn. Judging from the landscape, you'd have no idea that one of the greatest wonders of the world was just up ahead.

It occurred to me that the same may be true of our futures.

It's our choice how we spend our time during the "long drive"— the time we spend in the uncertainty of our various painful life circumstances. I could have decided there was no way the earth was suddenly going to quite literally split into a breathtaking canyon up ahead; I could have turned the car around and gone home. Being the rational academic I am, I could have justified my decision with the fact that there was no evidence during the long drive for this world-wonder supposedly up ahead.

But the dark isn't about gathering evidence. The dark is about trusting that what you need is up ahead and that who you are becoming requires you to be in the dark for a period of time. You are being shaped in the dark, and who you become is far more important than any particular life outcome because who you turn out to be will influence the rest of your life. I needed to keep my eyes on the road, follow the map, trust that I would reach my destination if I stayed the course, keep my hope and expectations up, and exhibit perseverance and patience despite the immediate evidence of my surroundings, or lack thereof. And because I did all that, I got to experience one of the most magical and majestic places on earth. We need to do the same when we're in the dark. Because the you that's up ahead is worth it.

Detach from the Outcome

Although we are not in control of the outcomes, we are in control of our choices and our responses. Ancient Buddhist wisdom teaches that we can reduce our suffering by detaching from outcomes. That doesn't mean we stop desiring an outcome (although some Buddhists may disagree with me here). To me it means that we no longer make our happiness contingent upon achieving that particular outcome. We'd like it, but we'd be okay without it, and we go on living our lives in the meantime. That's detachment.

When we're in this more detached place, we're still in a state of uncertainty because we don't know how it all turns out. But we're no longer governed by fear because the mind doesn't need to try to figure out how it works out or to make it all work out a certain way. When we're in this detached, more objective state of mind, we are better able to make values-based choices rather than emotional or pain-based choices.

You see, when we're grasping for a certain outcome—a certain way life "should" be—our choices are governed by our pain. We are living from one small, narrow perspective of what we think we need to be content, and we use our subsequent choices and actions to try to experience this one way of being, no matter what the cost. In contrast, when we make choices based on our values, such as peace, love, connection with others, and authenticity, we start to build and live a life worth living—even if we don't have what we think we want or need right now (i.e., that desired outcome). A life in alignment with our values is much more satisfying than a life spent trying to make things work out how we think they should. As you've probably noticed by now, our feeble attempts to control life don't work anyway.

You're in the Middle of Your Story

I'm a big fan of spoiler alerts. What's the point of going to the theater or buying the book if you already know how it all turns out? Sure, tease me with a little of the story, but don't ruin the fun by telling me how it ends! When it comes to my life, however, I want to know what's next. I want to know how it all works out, especially when I'm going through something difficult. I want to know not only that the pain is going to end, but also exactly when it's going to end. I want assurance that I've got a happy ending around the corner. I dislike being in the dark as much as the next person.

You're in the middle of your story. This was a phrase a friend of mine would remind me of often as I limped my way through the separation and the loneliness that followed. My mind would play with this phrase, hoping that it meant the separation was temporary and we'd get back to the original story—the till-death-do-us-part story. The longer the separation went on and the more detached my husband became, the more I had to rework the interpretation of this phrase.

Eventually, I realized that my story was so much more than the marriage story. The marriage was part of my life story, but only one part. As long as I made it THE story, I was stuck in despair and clinging desperately to a reality that no longer existed. When I was able to see that my marriage, and what likely would soon be my divorce, were elements of my story, albeit significant elements, my life took on a greater meaning. I was more than my marriage. I was more than a wife. My mission on earth encompassed more than devoting my life to being in partnership with this man. I still yearned for him to come home, but the intensity of this longing started to subside. I was still in the middle of my marriage story because the outcome was still an unknown. But more important, especially for my healing and recovery, was the understanding that I was still in the middle of my *life* story.

You are reading this book because you or someone you care about is in the middle of a story, a pain-and-suffering story. You likely want to know the specific ending of your story as much as I did. We want to get to the end—get out of the dark—as quickly as possible. No one wants to savor a difficult, painful story when they are the protagonist.

The Middle Is the Juicy Part

Let me tell you a little about what happens in the middle of stories and why being in the middle isn't such a bad thing. Stories are composed of a beginning, a middle, and an end. The beginning sets the stage, introduces us to the characters, and gets us intrigued enough to keep reading. The end is when we find out how things worked out for the characters and brings the story to a close. Those parts are pretty straightforward. The middle of the story is the meat. You might think of the beginning and the end of the story as the top and bottom halves of a bun sandwiching a juicy hamburger in the middle. We don't eat a hamburger for the bun; we eat it for the hamburger patty inside the bun. The bun just provides some structure around the meat, keeps it from dripping all over our lap, and helps keep all those yummy toppings in place.

If there was no middle of the story, there would be no reason to have a beginning or an end. There is no story without the middle part. The middle is where all the action happens. It's where we find out more about the characters, who they are deep down, what they like, who they love, and what they struggle with. The middle is where the conflict happens; it's where the challenges the characters must overcome are presented. It's when the story gets good and we have a hard time putting the book down to go to sleep at night. The middle is where the life work of the characters is revealed. It's when the characters are given a chance to become something more than they were when we first met them in the introduction. It's when they get the opportunity to become heroes.

The middle is why there is a story to tell in the first place.

Blooming Happens in the Middle of the Story

If you are in the dark right now, then you are in the middle of your story. And if you're in the middle of your story, then it's inevitable that you are going to experience conflict, pain, and challenges. That's just how the middle works. If we're lucky, we have periods of challenges interspersed with periods of rest and healing. For some of us, those rest and recovery periods feel few and far between. For all of us, this is our big chance. This is our chance to become more than we were in the earlier parts of our story. This is the time we get to set ourselves up for a truly satisfying ending.

Blooming in the dark happens in the middle of the story. And the middle of the story requires being in the dark because the middle means you don't know how it all works out in the end. But—and this is important—what happens in the middle determines what happens in the end.

For those of you who hate being in the dark about things as much as I do, I encourage you not to give up. Despite what it feels like right now—juicy, messy, confusing, painful—the middle is a precious time.

It's where you get to become the person you were designed to be. It's where you bloom in the dark.

Your Turn

With the following prompts, you will have the opportunity to journal about what it is like to be in the unknown, the middle of your story. The prompts are designed to help you develop another perspective about being in the dark; that is, how uncertainty about the ending can be a gift. You'll write about the life outcome(s) you desire and if and how you might detach some from these outcomes, so that you can begin crafting and experiencing a life worth living. Through writing about these prompts, you will work toward embracing being in the dark, rather than fighting against the uncertainty of it all, and explore how to establish a sense of trust, safety, and hope in the midst of uncertainty.

WRITING PROMPTS

Defining My Dark

What are you currently in the dark about? In other words, what are you uncertain about or what do you find yourself anxiously wondering about how it will work out?

How I Handle Being in the Dark

What has your experience of being in the dark (i.e., uncertainty) been like? Have you found yourself fighting against it, trying to figure things out or make things turn out a certain way? Or, have you made peace with it and accepted being in this state of unknowing? If you haven't made peace with it yet, what might help you to get there?

Dialogue with Uncertainty (i.e., Your Dark)

Pretend that Uncertainty isn't just a state that you are in, but a character in your life story. Have a conversation in writing with Uncertainty. To let Uncertainty speak, you might write this as a dialogue, play, poem, or story. Ask Uncertainty why it is here, what it has to say, and what it needs from you. Then listen and record what Uncertainty has to say to you. Uncertainty may have a few questions for you, too. Try answering those questions as if you are having a conversation.

Detaching

Are you attached to an outcome? Name it. What emotions come up as you think about detaching from this outcome? How does it feel emotionally to be grasping at this outcome? How does it feel mentally? Physically in your body? Spiritually? What do you need to feel more comfortable still desiring this outcome, yet also detaching from it (i.e., to no longer make your happiness contingent upon achieving this particular outcome)? What steps can you take to detach?

The Gift of Being in the Dark

How might being in this state of unknowing actually be helping you to bloom? Could being in the dark be a gift? What parts of your character are being developed?

The Middle of Your Story

What does the phrase "You're in the middle of your story" mean to you? Why do you think the middle requires being in the dark? What is one thing you need or one thing you could do to feel safer and less distressed and afraid of being in the middle?

Using the Middle of Your Story Well

Instead of focusing all of your attention on trying to figure out the ending of the particular story you are in right now, take some time to contemplate the opportunities you've been given here in the middle. How do you want to respond to these opportunities? What shifts will you need to make in order to make the most of the middle?

BLOOMING CHECK-IN

1. What came up for you as you completed your writing prompts in this chapter? What would you like to do with this information about yourself and your blooming process?

2. In what ways did you grow this week, even just a little bit? Did you make any changes? What are you proud of?

3. How will you continue to apply this blooming principle in your life?

BLOOMING TIP

There is a quote by the author Anne Lamott that I have found comforting during my times of uncertainty and unknowing. She said, *"It helps to resign as the controller of your fate. All that energy that we expend to keep things running right is not what keeps things running right."* When we are in the dark about an outcome, our tendency is to do whatever we can to try to control our fate. Embracing the idea that we're not in charge of our fate or our story in the first place is one way to relax our hold on life. How might this idea fit within your belief system? If it's not our energy that is keeping things running right, what or who does? I invite you to let your mind marinate on the notion of resigning as the controller of your fate. If this idea brings a sense of comfort or peace, consider putting in your resignation notice!

Night Bloomer: Kimberlie

Kimberlie is a single mother of three children and a therapist in private practice. Here is how she and her daughter bloomed in the darkness of mental illness.

"The past four years have been filled with many trials. In 2014, my then seventeen-year-old daughter tried to take her life. She was in a coma for three days. I was told she would die, be brain dead, or be hooked up to machines for the rest of her life. I'm divorced and found myself without any outside support. It was like people just didn't know how to handle this type of crisis. My family did not reach out either, which added to the feeling that God had given me too much to bear.

"It was nothing less than a miracle and answer to prayer when my daughter made a full recovery. The three neurologists were astounded when she woke up from the coma and was completely functional physically and mentally. I know it's rare to have a happy ending like this. However, that was not the end of the trial. She was hospitalized over thirty more times over the next few years. What we were going through crippled my ability to do much outside of maintaining my private practice to make ends meet financially and take care of my three children. I was either in the office seeing clients or at the hospital with my daughter.

"I am thankful to report that she is now a healing, maturing twenty-one-year-old. She is blessed with an incredible natural talent to draw and write. As a result of her struggles, she has begun using these talents to share about mental health issues. She also plays guitar and piano and writes her own songs, which she hopes God will use to touch the lives of those suffering with mental illness and trauma.

"I am also grateful for what God did within my own broken heart and exhausted emotions and body. I was devastated by what God allowed me to go through alone, as a mother and a woman. It seemed to never end. Many times, I felt like giving up and wondered why trials kept happening. I couldn't understand it. Talk about being in the dark. But I can honestly say that so much good has come from this heartbreaking time. On the other side of it, I now have a deep understanding of trauma, mood disorders, and abuse that I would never have had if we did not go through all this. I had to live it to really get it.

"I also speak and write about trauma and mental illness, something I hadn't done before, at least not with the knowledge and insight I do now. I'm also looking for work outside of private practice, so that I can do something larger for those who suffer. I'm a better therapist, mother, and woman as a result of the suffering we endured. Of course, I wish we never had to go through this. Yet, I also see the purpose and beauty that has emerged from this suffering, and I know there is more of both to come."

CHAPTER 5

EXPANDING COURAGEOUSLY

Today, will you choose courage or comfort? You cannot have both.
There is nothing comfortable about being brave with your life.

—Brené Brown

Are you courageous? When I ask my clients this question, almost all of them say no. Scared, anxious, afraid? Yes. Brave? No. Yet, if you had the privilege of hearing the things they are willing to talk about in session, the things they are willing to try or try again, and the ways they refuse to give up despite the enormity of their pain, you'd agree with me that each and every one of them qualifies as courageous.

It's not just my clients that I consider courageous. The very fact that you are reading this book, trying these journaling exercises, and engaging in the blooming process shows me that you're courageous, too. And that's good because as you've probably noticed, this process requires a lot of courage! Blooming is about growing and expanding, and change and expansion of any kind usually come hand in hand with some sort of fear or anxiety. To effectively face these inherent fears, we need courage. That's why I've called the fifth principle of blooming in the dark *Expanding Courageously.*

The good news is that we don't have to stop being afraid in order to be courageous. Listen to how our fellow Night Bloomer, Nelson Mandela, described what it means to be brave. And he should know;

he had to demonstrate courage almost every day of his life. He said, *"I learned that courage was not the absence of fear, but the triumph over it. The brave man is not he who does not feel afraid, but he who conquers that fear."*

Isn't that a relief? Not only do we not have to stop being afraid in order to be courageous, the truth is we can't be courageous unless there is something to fear. Fear is a necessary condition for courage! Think of fear like a setup for courage. So, we could say that courage is being afraid and doing it anyway.

That begs the question: *Why* do it anyway? It's not pleasant to face our fears. In fact, it can be one of the most uncomfortable things we do in life. Franklin D. Roosevelt answered the "why" question this way. He said, *"Courage is not the absence of fear, but rather the assessment that something else is more important than fear."* We choose to face our fears because we decide that what we want to achieve and who we want to become is more important than avoiding feeling afraid.

Feel Your Fear and Do It Anyway

For some of us, courage—being afraid and doing it anyway—means facing reality rather than embracing an illusion. For others, courage is simply getting out of bed in the morning. For others a little farther along in the healing process, courage means forging a new identity and expanding both internally and externally. This chapter will help you build your courage muscle and expand courageously, no matter how fearful you might feel right now as you contemplate your situation and your future.

Courage isn't a trait just needed by soldiers, firefighters, and others who face physical danger regularly. Each one of us is called upon in different ways to be brave in our own lives. Maybe being brave for you is finally standing up to your mother, or confronting the large debt you've accumulated, or speaking out against injustice, or asking for that long-overdue raise, or trying to have another child, or entering the dating world again after losing your spouse. Or maybe you've been diagnosed with a chronic illness or your child has made some poor life decisions. In these situations we have a choice about how we are going to respond. Will we crawl into bed and pull the covers over our head— literally or metaphorically—wishing and hoping that whatever we are facing will magically disappear? Or will we summon the courage to face that situation? Will we move forward even if we are afraid?

The lyrics of one of Lee Ann Womack's popular songs describe the attitude we all need to take when blooming in the dark. She says, "*When you get the choice to sit it out or dance, I hope you dance.*" A client of mine heard this song on the radio recently and chose the word "dance" as his blooming word for the year. I asked him what it meant to him and he said, "It means when life presents you with an opportunity, just do it, especially if you're afraid." If you've never heard the song *I Hope You Dance* or read the lyrics, I'd highly encourage you to do so. It captures the essence of what it means to be courageous after life has knocked you down.

Deprive Fear of Its Power

I've learned something interesting about fear as I've grappled with it in my own life and helped others to do the same. There is a paradox that fear tries desperately to hide from you because once you know it, you're well on your way to being free from it. Here it is: When you face the thing you're afraid of, either because it has happened or because you're willing to look closely at the possibility of its happening, fear wins the battle (i.e., you feel fearful), but in winning the battle it ultimately relinquishes the war (i.e., you realize you don't have to be fearful anymore). Fear blackmails us with various scary threats, often something like, you're not going to make it if X happens. So, we live in fear of X happening and we suffer every day trying to avoid this feared future. But when we call fear on its threat—when we courageously turn around and face what we fear head-on—we will feel afraid at first, but in doing so, we discover that fear's dreaded threat is an illusion and the bondage of fear is finally broken.

In other words, when you face your fear, you deprive it of the power to control your life thereafter. For me, my greatest fear was loving a man, making a till-death-do-us-part commitment, and then having him leave me. I watched this fear come true right before my eyes. Fear had told me all my life that I wouldn't make it if that ever happened to me, likely fueled by experiencing my parents' divorce as a young child. But little by little, make it I did. And then I realized it was all a big lie I had bought into—not being able to survive the loss of a great love. So, although it was painful to lose my marriage, I learned that particular fear was a powerful illusion that I had allowed to blackmail me for most of my adult life. As I stay conscious of this truth, fear no longer gets to control how or who or how much I love. The blackmail is over.

In the psychology world, facing your fear and thus depriving it of the power to control you is called exposure therapy. It's an excellent treatment for overcoming fear and anxiety. Essentially, in this treatment, you make small steps toward facing your greatest fears. Let's say you have a fear of snakes. Rather than starting off by putting a real live snake around your neck (did that thought give you goosebumps, too?), we'd start out with just the thought of a snake in your nearby vicinity or by placing a fake plastic snake on the other side of the room. We'd use various strategies, such as deep breathing, to help you experience a state of relaxation while in the presence of something you fear. This exposure experience helps retrain your brain so that it no longer perceives the thought of a snake in your vicinity or the presence of a fake snake as a danger. If there is no perception of danger, there is no feeling of fear.

Over time, as you take small steps toward the actual feared object or outcome (e.g., steps such as holding the fake snake or looking at a real snake in a secure container), we would gradually get you to the place where you are able to handle touching a real snake. It's a fascinating process to watch and has provided lasting freedom to many people who experience significant distress from their fears.

Stretch, but Don't Splatter

Now, the situation that brought you to this book was probably more like getting a dozen live snakes thrown at you all at once (or if snakes don't bother you, substitute in something that does terrify you). Looking ahead at your future and what you are being called upon to do in order to bloom may feel that way, too. When our lives get turned upside down, we often feel paralyzed by fear. This can become a vicious cycle of wanting to move forward, but feeling too afraid to do so. Our inability to make these desired changes causes us to feel depressed and down on ourselves, which makes us even more afraid that we'll never escape this misery.

To get out of this cycle, we're going to use the same principles of exposure therapy to help us move through our fear, take action, and expand courageously. We'll do it one small step at a time. By doing it in small intentional steps, your brain learns over time that it's not dangerous to expand, and the fear is never so much that it overwhelms and paralyzes you from taking action. I like to think of it as taking small calculated risks. As my life coach likes to say, it means we choose a course of action that is just risky enough that it will require us to be stretched, but not so big or risky that it causes us to splatter.

Speaking of taking action, there's some neat science that shows that taking active steps toward a desired goal helps to reduce depression and increases our confidence in ourselves. Moreover, when we do things that are novel and/or that are outside of our comfort zone, our brain releases important chemicals such as dopamine, which is our pleasure and reward neurotransmitter. It's the chemical that tells our brains, "This was good! We need to do this again!" Our behavior and our biology help to reinforce our desire and commitment to continue to expand courageously.

Your Turn

The following prompts are designed to help you draw upon your own internal well of courage to expand courageously. You will explore what courage means to you, what fears you need to face in order to grow, and how to flex your courage muscles. You'll write about what expanding courageously looks like in your life, including new hobbies you want to try and experiences you want to have, as well as what baby steps you need to get there. As you write, you will play with new identities you can grow into, one small stretch at a time.

WRITING PROMPTS

Getting Started: Mind Mapping

Write the word "courage" in the center of your page. Draw a circle around it. Then think of another word that you associate with courage. Write it somewhere near the word courage, draw a circle around it, and attach the two circled words with a line. Do this for as many words as you can think of that you associate with courage, drawing circles around the words and using lines to attach them to the original word "courage" in the center of the page. Then repeat this process for each of the new words you just wrote—thinking of words associated with these new words, drawing circles around them, and attaching these words together with lines. Do this for five minutes until you fill your page with an ever-expanding map or web of linked words.

After you read your mind map, write down what courage means to you. How would you define courage?

Naming Your Fears

Research in psychology has found that one way to lessen an emotion is to label it. There is something about naming an emotional experience that helps to diminish its intensity.

- Take a moment to name each of your fears.

- For each of those fears, what threat or blackmail message has fear given you?

- What is the opposite message? In other words, if you let courage speak up, what would it say about each of these fears?

Taking a Closer Look at Fear

Think about a situation you are concerned or anxious about right now. Write about that situation using several or all of the following prompts:

- What exactly are you afraid of?

- What is the worst possible thing that could happen? Is it really likely to occur?

- Where does this fear come from?

- How is fear holding you back?

- What would you do if you weren't afraid?

- What is that "something else that is more important than fear" for you?

- If you haven't been as courageous as you had hoped you might be, who or what might help you become more courageous?

- Have you been courageous in the past? Write about that time and what enabled you to be brave then. What happened as a result of your courageous acts at that time?

You may find that your subject changes as you write. That's actually helpful. Let yourself explore your thoughts and feelings by allowing your writing to take shape as you go. If you want, go through the questions again using another situation that you are anxious about.

My Courage Heroes

Write about one (or more) of your heroes or role models who has demonstrated courage in his or her life. What do you admire about this person? What has this person taught you about fear and courage? How has this helped in your current situation?

As a longer-term project, consider creating a "Courage Book." Try noticing and then writing down the everyday examples of courage that you see in yourself and in others. Perhaps your child stands up for herself when she thinks her teacher has been unfair. Perhaps you ask a colleague not to make remarks that you find offensive. Maybe you decide to sign up for dance lessons even though you feel kind of nervous about doing so. Perhaps a non-techie friend of yours gets brave enough to learn to use Twitter. Or maybe you read about how a seemingly confident and very talented performer copes with stage fright. When you have a day where you struggle to feel brave, read through the entries in your Courage Book. Let the courage of others and of yourself in the past inspire your courage now.

I Hope You Dance

If you haven't done so already, listen to Lee Ann Womack's song *I Hope You Dance*, or read the song lyrics. A quick search on the Internet will bring up both. Then respond to some or all of the following prompts:

- What does it mean to you to choose to dance rather than to sit it out in life?

- How do you feel when you think about choosing to "dance"?

- How do you feel when you think about sitting out?

- Where are you sitting out in your life?

- Where have you already begun to dance?

- Are you currently taking the path of least resistance? How is this working or not working for you?

- What chances or risks could you take right now? Why might they be worth taking?

My Blooming Expansion List

"He had found out that if he wanted to fly, he first had to jump."
—Nina George, The Little Paris Bookshop

Have a good look at your current activities. We often live on autopilot, doing the same things every day or every week that we've done for years. The problem with living this way is that we don't consider the fact that we may no longer really enjoy what we're doing. We're simply doing it because it's a habit. Take a moment to think about what you're doing in your life out of habit rather than pure enjoyment. Also look for the gaps. What aren't you doing that you wish you were?

Next, write a list of twenty-five activities that you have either always wanted to do or did at one time and enjoyed. These might be things such as see a movie, buy fresh flowers, take a pottery class, go on a girls' or guys' night out, go to a comedy show, learn how to sail, or travel somewhere new.

Beside each item, rank it on "stretchiness." A score of 1 would mean it stretches you only a little bit to engage in this activity; a score of 10 would mean that you can't imagine anything stretching you out of your comfort zone more than this activity.

Then, over the next few weeks and months, work your way through your blooming expansion list, item by item. Start with the activities you ranked with the lowest stretchiness score and work your way up. Remember, the goal is to stretch without splattering!

What I'm Proud of

Have you ever noticed that the closer the sun gets to setting, the more beautiful is the sky? Or how the leaves have never been more glorious than when they are dying in the fall? Beautiful things happen in the dark.

Take stock of the changes that have already happened in you and in your life since you began this blooming process. What are you proud of? What beauty is emerging in your life? What do you want to celebrate? How will you celebrate these changes?

BLOOMING CHECK-IN

1. What came up for you as you completed your writing prompts in this chapter? Did you notice where you feel fear in your body? What about where you feel courage?

2. In what ways did you grow this week, even just a little bit? Did you make any changes? What are you proud of?

3. How will you continue to apply this blooming principle in your life?

BLOOMING TIP

Ironically, sometimes what requires the most courage is allowing ourselves to feel good again. We get so used to feeling sad or lonely or afraid that it can almost be uncomfortable and anxiety provoking to feel joy, hope, love, and peace again. Hearing ourselves laugh after a loss can feel wrong, as if grieving and laughing aren't allowed to happen at the same time. The pain of loss and suffering causes many of us to guard our hearts against feeling positive emotions. The thought of losing these feelings a second time seems unbearable.

However, depriving ourselves of these positive emotions actually slows down our healing and blooming process. We need these positive emotional experiences more than ever during times of suffering. I invite you to look for ways that you are reluctant or fearful of feeling good. Then, see if you can start to expand in these areas, slowly giving yourself permission to feel those outlawed positive emotions. You might journal about what it's like to begin to experience these feelings again, what fears come up, and how you can continue to show courage in the face of those fears. A wise friend of mine once asked me, *What if the only thing you had to excel at was joy?* Consider this question as you're creating and executing the items on your Blooming Expansion List.

CHAPTER 6

KEEPING YOUR MIND ON BLOOMING

We become what we think about all day long.

—Ralph Waldo Emerson

You've probably heard the popular health adage "you are what you eat." It's true: The fuel we put into our body determines how our body runs and what building blocks are available for cellular growth, functioning, and repair. But food isn't the only thing we need to pay attention to if we want a healthy body and a productive life. We also need to pay attention to the thoughts we are feasting on all day and, sometimes, all night long.

Research has shown that just like food, our thoughts also provide physical building blocks for cellular development and functioning[39]. When we think a thought, our brain releases certain chemicals and electrical signals, which then have a significant influence on our brain and the cells of our body. When we think negative thoughts, such as sad, revengeful, or fearful thoughts, our brain releases chemicals that make our bodies feel poorly. Just think about how you felt the last time you were angry. If you're like most of us, your body felt tense, your heart beat faster, and you might have felt sweaty or dizzy, too.

Our brain releases different chemicals when we think positive, joyful, and peaceful thoughts. Consider how your body felt the last time you felt peaceful. You probably felt relaxed, your heart beat slower, and your breathing was deeper. The important point here is that our body reacts to every thought we think, and it does so automatically. When we're in a negative state of mind, we pay for it in more ways than one.

More so than at any other time, when we're in the dark, we need an abundance of healthy nutrients both to repair and to bloom. This means we need an abundance of positive, life-producing thoughts. You see, as Night Bloomers, we are more than what we eat: We are what we *think*. That's why the sixth blooming principle is called *Keeping Your Mind on Blooming*. We're going to look at three specific strategies we can use to harness the power of our mind to increase our blooming potential.

Use Your Mind to Re-Right Yourself

Humans are wired to be resilient. Homeostasis is an example of the brilliant internal programing we are born with that allows us to overcome challenges to our physiology, such as getting overheated or exhausted or sustaining an injury. I like to think of homeostasis as our re-righting tendency, like a boat that is able to stay afloat and upright on a choppy sea. We have internal mechanisms to re-right emotionally, too. These mechanisms develop over time, and some of us are better at using them than others. Think of the two-year-old who has a wailing, fist-pounding breakdown on the sidewalk when the ice cream slips off of her ice cream cone. She hasn't developed these emotional re-righting skills yet. Give her a few years, and she'll be upset about the ice cream, but not debilitated by it. That's because she's learned how to manage her emotions and bring herself back into emotional balance (i.e., self-regulation, something all children must learn).

However, when we experience loss or trauma, sometimes we get in our own way of re-righting. Indeed, the biggest blooming challenges we face are often internal, generated by our own minds. In this chapter, we'll look at three specific skills based on psychological science that will help us emotionally re-right ourselves. These skills help to change our mental state, so that we can get ourselves in alignment with our innate ability to re-right, grow, and transform. The three strategies are Intentionally Directing Your Attention, Changing Your Thoughts, and Feeding Your Hope. Each of these strategies is designed to give us greater control over our mental state, helping our minds to stay focused on what we really want: to bloom.

1. Intentionally Direct Your Attention

Your attention matters. Have you ever been driving down the highway when something caught your eye on the side of the road and before you realized it, your car was suddenly headed toward the ditch? You thought you were keeping your hands still on the wheel, but unconsciously you made subtle shifts such that you began driving in the direction you were looking. Those who ride motorcycles know all about the dangers of not looking where you want to go.

Our lives are like driving a car; they will go in the direction we're paying attention to.

When we've lost something or someone important to us, or things didn't work out as we had hoped, it's easy to get focused on the past. The problem is, to return to our driving metaphor, if we drive while looking into the rearview mirror for too long, we will eventually crash. Life is happening in front of us, not behind us. What we pay attention to is the direction in which we will go, whether that's the direction we wanted to head in or not.

In any moment, you have three choices for where you can put your attention: You can put it on the past, the present, or the future. If you're grieving or feeling depressed, your attention is likely on the past. If you're anxious or worried, you're likely focused on the future. The problem with these two choices is that neither of them actually exists. Neither is reality. The past has come and gone. The future hasn't happened yet. The only reality we have is the present moment. That's not to say that focusing our attention on memories is wrong, or that we shouldn't think about or plan for the future. Both have their place and both can bring us pleasure depending on what we are thinking about. What is critical is that we remember that in every moment we are making a choice about how we will spend our attention. Given that our lives follow our attention, we need to be wise and intentional spenders of our attention.

Your only reality is this moment, right now, which you are choosing to spend reading this book. My only reality right now is having this conversation with you, my fellow Night Bloomers, as I type this chapter. For those of you familiar with the term *mindfulness*, you'll recognize that training our minds to have a present-moment focus is the essence of cultivating mindfulness.

I recently heard someone say that we shouldn't focus on creating a better future. That caught my attention because I'd always thought focusing on creating a better future was a smart thing to do. He went on to explain that instead we should focus on creating a better present. When we do that, we still set ourselves up for the future we desire, but more importantly, we are able to actually experience the life we want in the present moment. Blooming happens in the present moment. Intentionally focusing on the present and how we can improve it is the best way to experience the life we desire and become the people we dream of becoming.

2. Change Your Thoughts

When you're in the midst of pain and suffering, it can feel like your life is being driven by your emotions. It's like a nightmare roller coaster with lower and lower dips and endless upside-down loops. Just when you think you're getting a handle on things, boom, something will remind you of what you lost or what you want but don't have, and suddenly you're back in a downward emotional loop. Our choices and behaviors become ruled by whatever emotional state we're in—and let's face it, when you're in the dark, those emotions usually aren't positive ones. We need to figure out how to get our emotions out of the driver's seat of our lives.

The thing is, our emotions aren't actually what is driving us, even though it feels that way. The truth is that our thoughts drive our emotions, which then drive our choices and behaviors. This is the essence of cognitive behavioral therapy or CBT, a type of therapy that has a lot of empirical support for treating mental health issues like depression and anxiety. CBT teaches that we need to change our thoughts in order to change our emotions.

It's next to impossible to will ourselves out of an emotion. But there are two effective ways we can change our emotions: by changing what we're thinking and by changing what we're doing. The blooming principle *Courageously Expanding* illustrated how we can change our behavior to change how we're feeling. The principle of *Keep Your Mind on Blooming* is about how we can change what we're thinking, so we can experience more uplifting emotions. We don't need to believe every thought we think!

Here's an example of what I mean by changing our thoughts. Let's say a woman's husband died a year ago and she is still feeling devastated by her loss. She might be *thinking*: "I'll never get over Mark. He was the love of my life. I'll never be happy again." How does this make her *feel*? Sad, lonely, and probably also fearful. So, what *behaviors* does she engage in? She might isolate herself at home, turn down offers to spend time with friends, and certainly keep herself from anything that might involve another man. These self-isolating behaviors lead her to *think*, "I really am all alone and I always will be." She *feels* even more depressed, lonely, and hopeless. This leads to more isolating *behaviors*, perhaps staying in bed or crying or overeating. Do you see the downward spiral she got herself into with the thoughts she was thinking?

Now, let's turn this around and create an upward spiral using the same principles. This time she might *think* to herself, "I really miss Mark. He was the love of my life. I don't like being alone all the time." This is still a realistic thought and not Pollyanna-ish (a fear many people have when they hear, "Just change your thoughts and you'll feel better!"). This thought might make her *feel* sad, but it doesn't cut off the possibility of ever moving forward in life and being happy again like her last thought did. These less negative feelings could lead to more positive *behaviors,* such as accepting a friend's invitation to go out one night so that she doesn't have to sit at home by herself. She might then *think,* "I still felt sad when I was with Maria, but it was nice not to be by myself. It felt good to laugh for a bit." She then might *feel* a little more hopeful and less lonely. As a result, she may be more likely to accept offers to go out with friends or to even initiate some herself, *behaviors* that will continue to improve her mood.

Once we have identified the negative thoughts that are causing us emotional distress, we need to challenge and change them. This gets us out of the negative spiral and puts us into a positive spiral. If we let our thoughts have free rein, we will begin to believe our thoughts, our body will react to them, and our life will go in the direction they dictate. If we "talk back" to our negative thoughts and become an active guardian of our mind, we take the power back to feel better and live the lives we desire.

I have two favorite questions to help challenge and change unhelpful, negative thinking. First, ask yourself, *Is this thought true?* If it's not true, then you need to come up with a thought that is true. Untrue thoughts have no place in a Night Bloomer's mind! Sometimes thoughts are true. For example, I really did get a poor performance review and I'm at risk of losing my job. Or, I have been diagnosed with a chronic illness that doesn't have a cure. The second question to ask yourself in these cases is, *Is this thought helpful?* In other words, is it helpful to be ruminating on this thought? Almost always the answer is, No, it's not helpful. In that case, shift your thinking to something else that is more helpful. This might be, what can I do differently at work going forward? Or, given

I have this chronic illness, what information and support do I need to best manage the situation?

We don't have enough space in this chapter to go into more detail about these concepts, but I will provide some helpful resources at the end for those of you who are interested in learning more about CBT and how to change your thoughts. In sum, the emotional roller coaster we often find ourselves on during the dark seasons in life begins in our minds. Wage the war here, and you will find your emotions taking their rightful place as passengers, not drivers, in your life.

3. Feed Your Hope

The last cognitive skill that will help you develop the principle of *Keep Your Mind on Blooming* is to feed your hope. Hope is a critical ingredient in letting go of the past and moving courageously into the future. As such, hope is a must for blooming in the dark. Hope is an emotion, but as we just learned, emotions are generated by a certain way of thinking. If we can practice engaging in a hopeful way of thinking, we will experience greater hope. The *Oxford English Dictionary* defines hope as "a feeling of expectation and desire for a particular thing to happen." Thus, hopeful thinking is a positive, curious, growth-minded type of thinking.

We've talked earlier in this book about the power of expectations and the importance of getting our hopes up. Here I want to provide a strategy for doing so. It's a strategy I learned from my writing coach when I was going through my separation. It was a lifesaver for me. Here it is: You need to do more "What if-ing." But not the kind of what if-ing you're likely doing right now. How many times have you said something like, What if I'm never happy again? What if I can't have another baby? What if we go bankrupt? What if treatment for the illness makes it impossible to work and we lose the house? What if no one ever loves me again? What if I can't do this?

We're really good at imagining the worst-case scenarios. As we just saw, when we focus our attention and our thoughts on these negative scenarios, our emotions, our behaviors, and our very lives begin to go in these negative directions. Instead of coming up with worst-case scenarios, I want you to begin to focus on best-case scenarios, or even just better-case scenarios. You can do this by changing your "what if" statements. Here are some examples: What if this turns out well for me? What if I go to bed with a smile on my face? What if there's another way of looking at this? What if this is the most beautiful thing that ever happened to me? What if love is right around the corner? What if I'm being prepared for something incredible? What if our needs are provided for? What if I'm not alone in this mess? What if I'm stronger than I think? What if I love the person I end up being as a result of going through this pain?

By asking "what if" in this manner, you create a little opening in your brain. You're not telling it something definitive, like I won't lose my job or I will love again, which could easily be rejected as not true. Instead, you're proposing a possibility for your mind to marinate on. Filling your mind with these positive, curious questions is a wonderful way to quickly generate a more hopeful state of being.

Your Turn

The following journal prompts will give you the opportunity to practice each of these three skills designed to help you keep your mind on blooming. You'll examine where you are spending the majority of your attention— on the past, present, or future. And you'll have the opportunity to begin building your present-moment, mindfulness muscle. You will then be guided through writing exercises that help you to identify, challenge, and change unhelpful thinking. This will help you to make choices and engage in actions that are based on your values and true desires, rather than on your emotions. Finally, you will write about ways to feed your hope, including creating a habit of positive what if-ing.

WRITING PROMPTS

Intentionally Direct Your Attention: How Are You Spending Your Attention?

On what do you find yourself spending the majority of your attention? Things that happened in the past, which includes the distant past (e.g., years ago) up to the very recent past (e.g., yesterday or a few hours ago); the present (i.e., what is happening right now); or the future, which again might be the distant future or the soon-to-be present, like tomorrow? Think of your attention like a hundred-dollar bill. Estimate how you typically divide up that hundred dollars between the past, the present, and the future.

- What feelings and thoughts come up for you as you think about the way you spend your attention?

- Would you like to make any changes to the way you spend your present moment?

- What are these changes, and what are one or two small steps you could begin taking today?

Intentionally Direct Your Attention: Practicing Mindfulness

Pick one small thing that you want to become more mindful of for a few minutes every day. It doesn't have to be anything significant. This is just an exercise to begin training your mind to pay attention to the present. Perhaps you want to commit to paying attention to brushing your teeth every morning or mindfully washing the dishes after dinner or saying goodnight to your children. Describe the activity that you will bring your mindful attention to. Use this log to write down your reflections of what it was like to be simply present in the moment with all of your attention on this one thing for a few minutes each day. Do this for at least a week. Then answer the following questions:

- What did you learn?

- What surprised you?

- What changes will you make based on this experience with mindfulness?

My Mindful Activity is:

Reflections on my mindfulness practice:

Change Your Thoughts: The "Three Cs"

Try working through the following three steps for a situation that is upsetting you. The clue that you're thinking negative or unhelpful thoughts is usually experiencing a negative emotion, such as feeling sad, hopeless, angry, or anxious. You can work through these three steps every time you notice yourself stuck in a negative emotion.

1. Catch Your Thought:

My thought, belief, or expectation:

How this thought makes me feel:

How I behave when I think and feel this way:

2. Challenge Your Thought:

Is it true? Is it helpful? What evidence do I have that this is true? What evidence do I have that this is not true?

3. Change Your Thought:

What else can I tell myself? What is the truth? What is a more helpful way of thinking about this?

Change Your Thoughts: My Story Two Ways

What story have you been telling yourself about your time in the dark? This might be a story about what led you into this time of pain and suffering. Or, it might be a story about another challenging life situation that brings up negative emotions or doesn't feel resolved.

Take the next ten to fifteen minutes to write a few paragraphs describing your story. Include facts, feelings, thoughts, and explanations.

Once you are finished, try writing your story from another perspective. The perspective you might take is that of yourself already fully bloomed. What would your story look like from that vantage point? Below I provide an example of one of my own blooming stories. As you read it, notice the different way I frame the events that occurred. What emotions come up for you after reading my first story? What emotions come up after reading the second?

Now try it yourself. Remember to include facts, feelings, thoughts, and explanations, but this time from the perspective of your already beautifully bloomed self.

Michelle's Story, Two Ways

> **Story 1:** In 2005, I became inexplicably sick. I had just started my internship at Duke University Medical Center. It was the last required clinical practice year before I could receive my PhD. I had already successfully defended my dissertation. It was September. I was ten months away from achieving one of my life dreams. Then I started not to function. It started out with fatigue that quickly progressed. I would go home at lunch to try to sleep for half an hour, then come home after work, eat dinner, and go to bed. Weekends were spent in bed trying to get ahead of the fatigue. I saw doctor after doctor. No one knew what was wrong with me. All my blood work came back normal. One endocrinologist told me to take a nap, as if

that was the missing piece. By November, I couldn't get out of bed. I had to drop out of my internship.

I finally got diagnosed with adrenal fatigue by an integrative medicine physician. And then I got mono and strep throat on top of it. I spent the next seven months in bed. I thought I was dying. Nothing was helping. I was in such despair there were days I wondered if I wanted to keep trying. I couldn't do the most basic tasks. It didn't look like I was going to be able to finish my internship or my PhD. When I finally was able to go back the following year, I had to start over again with a new class of interns. I was the one who hadn't been able to cut it the first time. The Yale graduate student who couldn't even get through her internship. What a fraud.

Story 2 (From a Bloomed Perspective): In 2005, I became inexplicably sick. I had just started my internship at Duke University Medical Center. It was the last required clinical practice year before I could receive my PhD. I had already successfully defended my dissertation. It was September. I was ten months away from achieving one of my life dreams. Then I started not to function. It took a long time for a doctor to figure out what was wrong with me. This is how I was introduced to integrative medicine; conventional medicine hadn't helped. I didn't know there was another way of looking at health and treating patients. I took lots of supplements and herbs instead of medications. I learned the impact stress has on the body. I learned how to meditate. I took two intensive mind-body stress reduction classes at Duke. I deepened my spiritual practice.

I was the patient instead of the provider and I learned so much more than I had been learning in my internship.

I learned things that I would practice for the rest of my life, things I would teach my clients, and things I would teach other up-and-coming health care providers. I was able to return to my internship a year later and completed it successfully. I even finished my postdoc work early and became a professor at the same time my peers in my first internship class got their first faculty positions. Not only hadn't I wasted any time, but I learned so much that I never would have learned without this confusing and debilitating illness. I developed a closer relationship with God and now live a much healthier and more balanced lifestyle. Part of my life mission has become to pay this forward. Now I direct an integrative health and wellness graduate program, run wellness workshops, and practice integrative psychotherapy.

Feed Your Hope: Best-Case Scenario

We spend a lot of our mental energy worrying about the worst-case scenario. We imagine that if we plan for the worst, we will somehow be better prepared for it. Unfortunately, not only are we no more prepared for this feared situation, but we also make ourselves miserable in the process. Most of the time, what we worry about never happens! Rather than imagining the worst-case scenario, we can use our minds to do the opposite: imagine the best-case scenario. Take some time to write about the very best way your current circumstance (or life) could go. Be as detailed as you can. Then write about how you feel dwelling on the best-case scenario.

Feed Your Hope: What If?

What if you could use your words to create what you desire instead of what you fear? Try writing five to ten sentences that start with the words "What if …?" Have a look earlier in this chapter for examples.

What if ...? _____

What if ...? _____

What if ...? _____

What if ...? _____

What if ...? _____

BLOOMING CHECK-IN

1. What came up for you as you completed your writing prompts in this chapter? In what ways did you find yourself partnering with your mind and/or fighting against it?

2. In what ways did you grow this week, even just a little bit? Did you make any changes? What are you proud of?

3. How will you continue to apply this blooming principle in your life?

BLOOMING TIP

If you enjoyed the cognitive strategies in this chapter and would like to dive deeper into these concepts, there are a number of excellent books and workbooks you can purchase.

To train your attention and learn more about mindfulness:

- *Mindfulness for Beginners* by Jon Kabat-Zinn

- *Mindfulness in Plain English* by Bhante Henepola Gunaratana

- *Buddha's Brain: The Practical Neuroscience of Happiness, Love, and Wisdom* by Rick Hanson

- *The Precious Present* by Spencer Johnson

To learn more about changing your thoughts:

- *You Are What You Think* by David Stoop

- *The Feeling Good Handbook* by David Burns

- *Change Your Brain, Change Your Life* by Daniel Amen

- *Train Your Mind, Change Your Brain* by Sharon Begley

- *Rewire Your Brain: Think Your Way to a Better Life* by John Arden

These are excellent in-depth resources to learn more about how you can use mindfulness and change your thinking style to effect positive change in your life. That said, there are times when books like these are not enough. If you feel like you have lost control over your thoughts, or you're in a deep thinking rut and unable to get out on your own, or you've been unable to lift your mood after a long period of time, you would likely benefit from working with a therapist who offers cognitive behavioral therapy. One way to find a CBT therapist in your area is by searching for one on these websites: http://www.findcbt.org/xFAT/ and http://www.nacbt.org/find-a-therapist/

Night Bloomer: Oprah Winfrey

Life for Oprah Winfrey, one of the most powerful and influential women in the world, began in the dark. She was raised in poverty; grew up feeling unwanted after being passed back and forth between her mother, grandmother, and father; endured regular beatings; and was sexually abused by several family members. She reported becoming sexually promiscuous in her adolescence as a result of the abuse and found herself pregnant at age fourteen. Her baby boy died just weeks after he was born, a secret she kept in shame for many years.

Her struggles continued into early adulthood as she began her career. Hired to be an evening news anchor in Baltimore, she lost this job after a few months. Told she was "unfit for TV," she was demoted to writing and street reporting. As a reporter, she was reprimanded for being too slow with the copy and too compassionate and involved in her stories.

Yet, we all know Oprah's story doesn't end here. Rather than letting the painful events of her childhood and the failures of her early career define her, she used them to find her voice and her purpose in life. Indeed, she has been quoted as saying, "The greatest discovery of all time is that a person can change his future by merely changing his attitude."

The results of Oprah's blooming attitude and intention have been exceptional. She created an incredibly successful daytime talk show, *The Oprah Winfrey Show*, which aired from 1986 to 2011. She was a millionaire by age thirty-two; has a monthly magazine called *O, The Oprah Magazine*; owns her own TV channel, called OWN; has her own podcasts; has produced films and a Broadway musical; and was nominated for Best Supporting Actress for her role in *The Color Purple*. *Life* magazine named her the most influential woman and most influential black person of her generation. She was also named the "world's most powerful woman" by Time.com and CNN.

The darkness was a fertile place for Oprah, providing gems she would use to propel herself forward into the life of her dreams. Her media success was arguably in large part because the American public saw her as "one of us." Her experience of and transparency about her own painful struggles, losses, and failures made her authentic and relatable. It also created a deep well of empathy that is palpable when she speaks with her guests and audience members. A theme in Oprah's work and life mission is that of using her experiences in the dark to help inspire others to keep moving through and out of their own darkness. Indeed, two of her life mottos are "Nothing is ever wasted in life" and "Life is working for you, not against you."

Oprah's father seemed to have empowered her with the night blooming message in her mid-adolescence. In an interview, Oprah said, "My father turned my life around by insisting that I be more than I was." And is she ever. Oprah's life is an inspirational picture of what blooming in the dark can mean—not just for an individual, but also for the millions of people her life has touched.

CHAPTER 7

WRESTLING WITH THE DIVINE GARDENER

He has led me and brought me into the darkness, not light.
—LAMENTATIONS 3:2

It happened forty-five minutes after I got up off my knees in my home office. With my hands held up in surrender, I had said a three-sentence prayer: "God, we're making a mess of our marriage. We need your help. I give you this marriage." I certainly wasn't planning on having an *Eat Pray Love* moment, but that's what it turned out to be. I went and lay down on our bed and tried to read. I thought about how my husband and I had argued on the way home from church that morning, and feeling conflicted, I went down to the kitchen where he was making himself a snack. I apologized for being short with him, and told him how much I had been missing him and had been for a very long time. He made some sort of grunting noise to acknowledge that he had heard me and went back to making his snack. I trudged back upstairs, my heart heavy.

Not long afterward, he came up and asked me to talk with him in the living room. Hope surged through my body. Finally, we were going to discuss the distance in our marriage and how we were going to resolve it. I settled myself on the loveseat and then listened in shock as he calmly told me he didn't love me anymore and hadn't for a very long time, wasn't interested in trying therapy, had found an apartment, and was moving out in two weeks. He was done. I sat there stunned, trying desperately to figure out what was happening. I had asked God for his help just forty-five minutes earlier. What kind of God answers a sincere prayer for help with a divorce decree?

Being in the dark doesn't just impact us emotionally, mentally, and physically. For many of us, being in the dark also rocks us spiritually, sometimes to the very core. Indeed, spiritual struggles and spiritual pain is a common phenomenon among those going through difficult life circumstances. People often begin to question spiritual beliefs they once held dear, such as "God will never give me more than I can bear," "God helps those who help themselves," and even "God loves me."

At times, these spiritual struggles are so intense and so life-shattering that some people lose their faith in the dark. They can't find a way to fit what they've experienced into their belief system, and so they need to radically change or abandon their belief system to find a sense of integrity within. Yet, interestingly, others have the opposite reaction: They find their faith strengthened in the dark. These people report that their faith was the major thing that got them through to the other side.

No matter where you are on this spiritual continuum, this chapter is for you. We'll be exploring the seventh principle of blooming in the dark, called *Wrestling with the Divine Gardener*. I'm using the phrase "Divine Gardener" to refer to the sacred, transcendent dimension in life, whether you call this being or force God, the Divine, Source, Energy, Higher Power, or something else. At times, I will interchange the phrase Divine Gardener with God and use the male pronoun (he/his) for ease of writing, but please substitute the word and pronouns that fit best for you and your spiritual or religious beliefs. This chapter is meant to be inclusive, and my hope is that you find refuge and healing in these words and writing prompts.

Spiritual Pain Is Real, and it's Serious

Although spiritual pain is real, there is a tendency for us to keep it to ourselves. It just feels so intensely personal. It can also feel shameful to admit that we are having spiritual struggles, especially if the social norms in our faith tradition are that "good" [fill in the blank with your spiritual or religious tradition] don't get mad at God or don't get depressed or don't have spiritual doubts. Spiritual pain and struggle can then become an even lonelier wilderness to traverse because of our self-imposed, and sometimes other-imposed, silence and isolation. The experience of loss and tragedy may cause us to ask God why he let it happen. Some individuals feel their suffering is a punishment from God for some wrongdoing they feel they must have committed. Others feel abandoned by God, thinking that if God really loved them he would not have let this awful thing happen. Still others reject the notion of a God altogether after experiencing loss.

Researchers have studied spiritual pain and struggles for several decades. They have found that spiritual struggles—defined as tension or conflict regarding matters of the sacred—seem to fall into one of three main categories: divine, intrapersonal, and interpersonal[38]. In other words, we can have struggles with God or the divine, such as "Why did God let this happen?" or "God has abandoned me"; struggles within ourselves, such as doubt or guilt; and struggles with others about spiritual matters, such as experiencing conflict or judgment from others regarding our spiritual practices or beliefs.

Experiencing spiritual struggles during times of stress is very common. The science also shows that the more spiritual struggles people have, the more likely they are to also feel depressed and anxious, report lower quality of life, and even have an increased risk of mortality over a two-year period[41]! The empirical evidence is clear: For the sake of our mental and physical well-being, not to mention our spiritual well-being, we need to take spiritual struggles seriously.

What This Chapter Will and Won't Do

At one time or another, many of us have asked the question, "If there is a God, why does he let bad things happen, especially to good people?"

There are many books that delve deeply into theological explanations for this question. The purpose of this chapter is not to be a theological exposé. I couldn't even begin to do this question justice, given the diversity of religious and spiritual teachings on why people suffer. Instead, the purpose is the same as every other chapter: to propose that there may be another way to look at the suffering we experience, one that facilitates our growth and transformation. This time we'll be looking at it from a spiritual growth perspective.

Let me begin by being transparent and stating upfront two important points about myself: I believe in a good God. And I don't know why he lets people suffer. I have my ideas and hypotheses, but there are some events that are so awful and so disturbing that I find myself without any satisfying answers. I do have a spiritual perspective on suffering that has brought me, and many of the clients I have worked with, great comfort. I offer that to you here as one possible perspective. I know that for some this perspective will help you quiet the relentless struggle in your minds for meaning and peace. Yet, I also know that for others, the struggle for meaning will continue. If you are in the latter group, I pray you continue to seek the healing balm you need for your spiritual pain from other sources.

The Veiled Goodness of the Vinedresser

I want to use the picture of a vineyard to illustrate one potential spiritual perspective on suffering. It's a perspective that raises the possibility of the goodness—albeit the often veiled and confusing goodness—of the Divine Gardener. Have you ever been to a vineyard? If you have, you have likely gazed down long, straight rows of tangled, lush green vines and smelled the sweet aroma of ripening grapes. Standing among the vines, one has a sense of vitality and fullness. That is, you would have if you visited the vineyard in the summer.

The vineyard is a very different-looking place in the fall and winter. A desolate, barren place. What I find even more striking is that the vinedresser, the individual who takes care of the vines and harvests the grapes, appears to have a disturbing personality change with the seasons. All spring and summer, he treats the vines with love and pride. He is kind and attentive. The vines are his life, and he toils for hours to keep them healthy and safe, so that they have the best chance of growing strong and fruitful. In the late summer/early fall, during the harvest, the vinedresser carefully plucks the ripe fruit he has nurtured for months.

Yet, after the grapes are harvested from the vines, that same loving vinedresser then takes the pruning shears or handsaw and ruthlessly chops off great portions of the vine. The carnage is vast. The naked vine is reduced to a small, decimated version of its former glory. An onlooker not familiar with the care of a vineyard would no doubt wonder how the vinedresser could treat so harshly the vines that just gave him a bountiful harvest of grapes, a harvest sustaining his very livelihood. The vinedresser seems callous and cruel, if not completely mad.

When I visited a vineyard in North Carolina, I wanted to learn more about how the grapes are grown. The owner of the vineyard walked me down the rows of vines, heavy with the ripening harvest, as he explained the process. He told me that the reason why his grapes grew larger and better tasting every year was not because of the soil or the rain or even the sunshine, although these all played an important role. "No," he said, "the most important part of growing grapes is what happens after the harvest. It's the pruning I do every winter that ensures a better harvest every summer. The biggest mistake novice vinedressers make is not cutting off enough of the vine."

I learned that each year, vines have to be trimmed judiciously; the branches cut into and cut off, so that they can produce more fruit the following season. A loving vinedresser prunes his vines. A lazy vinedresser, one that does not care about the condition of the vine or the fruit it will produce, leaves the vine alone. In other words, the vine that is loved is put through pain. The vine that is loved suffers. It loses part of itself. The vine that is not loved is left alone and allowed to be comfortable and content.

The Divine Gardener's Loving Intention Is for Us to Grow

Has it felt like the Divine Gardener has taken the pruning shears, or perhaps a machete or hacksaw, to your life? It has sure felt like that in my life at times. And yet, I also feel a gentle nudging to consider the idea that the pain and suffering we endure in the dark seasons in life has behind it a loving intent. That perhaps the Divine Gardener allows painful circumstances, situations, and people not because we have done something wrong or have been abandoned or because the Gardener is callous or negligent. But rather perhaps these things are allowed because we *are* loved and so that we can become even more than we were before. Of all parties involved in the blooming process, it makes sense to me that the Gardener would want his flowers to have the biggest, brightest, most beautiful blooms possible. And as the Gardener, he knows exactly what it will take to get us there. The question is, can we trust the Gardener even when—especially when—what's happening in our lives doesn't make sense?

I've said it before and it bears repeating: I do not think the traumatic things that happen to us are good. The fact that there may be a loving intent behind the pruning in our lives does not make the pruning itself good, nor does it lessen the pain. It doesn't make atrocities right or loss something to be desired. Earlier we discussed the idea that nothing is ever wasted in our lives. I personally don't believe the Divine Gardener purposes to cause us pain and suffering. Instead, I believe the Divine Gardener uses everything that happens to us—pain and suffering included—to grow and transform us, not to destroy us. As Gardener, he knows our potential. He sees us in our fully bloomed and beautiful state. We see an awful mess, a terrible and unfair loss, a character that needs a lot of work, a situation that looks bleak. We feel pain that grips us to our very core. And sometimes we interpret our suffering as the

Divine Gardener having left us, or at least not caring about us because he allowed something bad to happen to us.

Similarly, it would be easy for the branches of the vine to interpret the vinedresser's pruning the same way. Think of the searing pain of being cut in half, and this after having done your best to please the vinedresser with a bountiful harvest. However, if the branch knew the vinedresser and his intention behind the painful action, the branch would understand that everything the vinedresser did to the branches was for their and the vineyard's ultimate good. The branch would trust the vinedresser, even when it didn't understand what the vinedresser was up to. Even when the vinedresser did something that caused it great pain.

So, it makes me wonder: Could the Divine Gardener be up to the same thing when our lives are being pruned in the dark?

Darkness Allows Us to Get to Know the Gardener

The only way for us to trust the Divine Gardener when we are going through our own private hell is if we know him. What is the Gardener's character? What is his intent toward me? Only then will we resist the temptation to forfeit the painful pruning process. In the dark, we get to know ourselves and what we are capable of in a new way. Similarly, one of the gifts we receive in the dark is the opportunity to get to know the Gardener in ways not possible in the light.

Just as it took the fall and winter seasons to see a different side of the vinedresser—a lover of the vine who was more interested in long-term gain over short-term comfort—so too there are aspects of the Divine Gardener that simply cannot be seen or experienced in the light. In the light, I knew the Divine Gardener as a loving being who cared about me, communicated with kindness and humor, and inspired great joy and peace. Yet, in the darkness of my deepest pain, the Divine Gardener revealed himself to me as husband, mother, healer, provider, deliverer, friend, comforter, and counselor. It occurred to me that these are aspects of God that I could only see and experience in the dark. My needs and experiences in the light are different than they are in the dark and, as a result, the way I interact with God is different too. I learned that the fertile covering of darkness was an invitation to intimacy with the Gardener that was not possible in the light.

The divorce became one of the most beautiful things that has ever happened to me. I have silently thanked my ex-husband many times over the last few years for releasing me. I am even more grateful that the Divine Gardener chose to answer my three-sentence prayer (not to mention all the daily prayers said over the next year for the restoration of my marriage) in his own way, not according to what I thought I wanted and needed. I realized later that all of the nos were in service of the one great big yes, and that great big yes was me— fully bloomed me.

Engage with the Questions

Don't get me wrong, it took me a long time and a lot of wrestling to get to this place of peace. I had to go from asking the Divine Gardener, "Why did you let this happen?" to "How do you intend to use this? What is the higher perspective here, the sacred perspective?"

The well-known quote by Rainer Maria Rilke is fitting in this context: "Be patient toward all that is unsolved in your heart and try to love the questions themselves, like locked rooms and like books that are now written in a very foreign tongue. Do not now seek the answers, which cannot be given you because you would not be able to live them. And the point is, to live everything. Live the questions now. Perhaps you will then gradually, without noticing it, live along some distant day into the answer."

I have found that one of the ways to move through spiritual suffering is to ask the questions and to fully engage with them. Giving ourselves permission to wrestle with the Divine Gardener in the dark is part of what it means to engage the questions. I've heard that one of the signs that a relationship is over is the feeling of indifference. If someone is angry or frustrated or distressed, they're still engaged. They still care. Indifference means someone has given up. They've stopped caring.

The Divine Gardener is not afraid of or offended by your anger or despair or doubt or fear. Your emotions and your thoughts are not a surprise to him, and they are not bigger than his loving intent for your healing, growth, and transformation. I believe engaging with the questions, feeling and expressing our emotions, while acknowledging our limited perspectives, and wrestling with the Divine Gardener are ways that can deepen and expand our spirituality in ways not possible in the light.

Your Turn

In the writing prompts below, you will have the opportunity to grapple with the discrepancy between what you have believed about the Divine Gardener and your challenging life experiences. Here you have the chance to wrestle with the Divine Gardener and safely and fully express any of the emotions you might be feeling, such as anger, despair, and resentment. This writing process will give you the chance to say things you may not feel comfortable sharing with others. These writing exercises will also open up a space for you to stand back and be curious about what the Divine Gardener may be doing in your darkness and how he may be revealing himself in new ways. The writing prompts will provide you with an opportunity to explore and develop an expanded understanding of who your Divine Gardener is and what he is doing in your life during this time.

Note that if you do not identify as spiritual or religious, you can skip these writing prompts, interpret the "Divine Gardener" in a way that better fits with your belief system, and/or modify the writing prompts however you like.

WRITING PROMPTS

The Discrepancy

How has being in the dark impacted your spiritual well-being, beliefs, and practices? Have you experienced a discrepancy between what you believed about the Divine Gardener and your challenging life experiences? What spiritual beliefs have you begun to question?

Take as much time as you need to answer these questions. You can also write about any other spiritual struggle you are experiencing. Acknowledging the struggle and grappling with the discrepancies is the first step in moving through it.

My Lament

A lament is an age-old way individuals across many faith traditions have expressed their pain and suffering to and about God. The page is a safe place to fully express all of the emotions you might be feeling, such as anger, despair, and resentment toward God, others, and/or yourself. Let this lament be the place where you give yourself permission to say things you may not feel comfortable sharing with others. Also, give yourself permission to wrestle with the Divine Gardener here—to pour out your pain, your grief, your doubt, your questions, your despair, and anything else that might be coming up for you.

The Vinedresser and the Vine

What was your reaction to the metaphor of the vineyard and the vinedresser? Did this perspective resonate? Why or why not? Do you feel like your life is being pruned? What meaning do you make of this pruning?

Who is the Divine Gardener in the Dark?

See if you can take a step back from your situation for a moment and enter a place of curiosity. If you had to guess, what do you think the

Divine Gardener might be doing in and with your darkness? What aspects of the Divine Gardener are being revealed to you in the dark that were not visible in the light?

Dialogue with the Divine Gardener

When we are in the dark, we often ask, "Why me?" or "Why did you let this happen?" Take the next ten or fifteen minutes and ask the Divine Gardener this question instead: "How do you intend to use this? What is the higher perspective here, the sacred perspective or purpose?" It might help to first spend a few minutes in quiet reflection, meditation, or prayer, during which time you ask your question and listen for a response. Sometimes the response feels loud and clear, and sometimes it feels like a gentle impression or feeling sense in your heart. Sometimes the response comes in the form of a picture. When you're ready, open your eyes and write down what you heard or felt.

Living the Questions

What does it mean to you to "live the questions"? What questions are you living? What would it take for you to fully engage the questions? How would doing so benefit you?

BLOOMING CHECK-IN

1. What came up for you as you completed your writing prompts in this chapter? How does wrestling with the Divine Gardener manifest in your thoughts, emotions, and body?

2. In what ways did you grow this week, even just a little bit? Did you make any changes? What are you proud of?

3. How will you continue to apply this blooming principle in your life?

BLOOMING TIP

As helpful as journaling about our spiritual pain and struggles can be, sometimes we need the witnessing presence or wise guidance of another person to fully address our spiritual pain. If this is you, I invite you to find a clergy member, spiritual leader, spiritual director, or a therapist trained in dealing with spiritual struggles and existential issues. These professionals are trained to listen, provide compassion (not judgment), and counsel that will both legitimize your spiritual pain and help you to find a path through it. Spiritual pain is real and it's serious, but it doesn't have to be part of your life forever. The dark night of the soul, as St. John of the Cross called it, is a dark *night*, not a dark forever. May the loving intent of the Divine Gardener be a light for your path.

CHAPTER 8

FERTILIZING WITH LOVE AND GRATITUDE

Love never fails.

—First Corinthians 13:8

As you know well by now, blooming in the dark isn't an overnight experience. Just as in nature, blooming is a process, and for many of us it's a long and challenging process. Although we can't just up and decide one day that we're fully bloomed any more than we can decide that the cake we put in the oven ten minutes ago is fully baked, there are a few things we can do to accelerate the process. I call these our blooming fertilizers. These are mindsets and actions that we can engage in to supercharge our transformation. There are many such fertilizers, but in my opinion love and gratitude are the most potent. In this chapter, on the eighth principle of blooming in the dark, we explore what it means to *Fertilize with Love and Gratitude*, why these powerful accelerators work, and how to use them in your own blooming process.

What's Love Got to Do with It?

The subject of love has dominated literature, poetry, music, and art for centuries. I want to take a slightly different angle. I want talk about love in the dark. Not the lights-are-out-and-you-are-with-your-sweetheart kind of love in the dark. I'm talking about love when our lives have just fallen apart. Love when we have been emptied of everything that gave us meaning. Love when we're limping through our days, when we're crawling through our job responsibilities, when we've lost the reason to get out of bed in the morning. Love in the dark, painful, agonizing periods of life. There is nothing romantic about this kind of love. This kind of love is hard.

Think about a time when you fell in love. Remember all the nice things you did for your beloved? You were probably trying to outdo one another, figuring out what made the other smile, and then doing that thing as well and as often as you could. You did this because you thought the world of this person. You didn't mind sacrificing your time, spending your money, or doing the extra chores because it gave you pleasure to see your beloved smile.

Now think about the person who irritates you the most or the person who has hurt you the deepest. For some of you, it's the same person you just thought about a moment ago. How many nice things do you feel motivated to do for this person? How much time do you sacrifice, money do you spend, and extra burdens do you take on for this person who is making your life miserable? I'm willing to bet not much, if any at all. We don't write poetry full of sweet nothings to our enemies.

It's easy to love when we're being treated well and when we're loved back. Loving someone who has wounded us or who makes our life challenging is a whole different story. Yet when we are rejected, when we are abandoned, when we are despised, when we are lied about, when we are gossiped about, when we are fired, when we are cheated on, when we are evicted, when we are treated unjustly—these are our greatest opportunities to respond in love. I don't know about you, but I'm not usually feeling very loving at these times! In fact, if I'm hurting, I'd rather be the recipient of love instead of being the one who responds in love. So, why am I suggesting that it's important that we make the choice to extend love when we're in the dark?

Loving Changes the Lover

Here's why: Because love is your secret weapon in the dark. It's the special sauce. It's the turbo charger. Indeed, according to many spiritual traditions, love is the most powerful force in the universe. Why do we need to love in the dark? Because love is the best fertilizer we've got, and the more we use it, the easier this transformation will be.

Now let me be clear. We don't love to get; we love to become. In my personal and clinical experience, I have noticed that loving doesn't necessarily change our situation or other people, or even get us the outcome we desire. Rather, *loving changes the lover.* In other words, loving changes you. And this, in my opinion, is one of the most beautiful aspects of blooming in the dark.

I learned this profound truth during my own blooming in the dark process. For weeks after my husband said he was leaving, I would get down on my knees every day and ask the Divine Gardener to love my husband through me with his love. I asked many times a day that I would become a woman who loved courageously, much, and well. God might not have answered many of my prayers how I wanted during that time, but he answered these. I loved that man with everything within me. I loved him in ways I hadn't even demonstrated when we were in the euphoric, nothing-could-be-better-than-this stage of our relationship. I loved my husband like I had never loved before.

Something remarkable started happening almost immediately after I began asking to be a vessel of love. I started changing inside, and these changes were manifesting in my attitude and my behavior. I wasn't *trying* to love, I wasn't grudgingly forcing it. I was genuinely loving my husband, the man who wanted nothing to do with me. You have to know this felt crazy to me. Instead of bitterness, anger, or resentment, emotions I fully expected to be feeling during that time, I felt love, respect, and tenderness. It was astonishing. In retrospect, I believe choosing to love him was one of the major reasons I was able to function as well as I did and why I was able to move through the divorce without any lingering resentment or anger.

I thought that loving my husband with all of me was going to soften his heart and save our marriage. Just the opposite happened, actually. The more I loved him, the harder his heart became and the harsher the things he said about me. Loving didn't change my circumstances. It didn't change my husband (at least not in ways that were visible to me). Loving changed me, the lover. I have never experienced anything like it.

We Are Living Conduits

You see, just like flowers that take up nutrients through their roots and stems, we too are living conduits: What flows through us permeates into us and changes us. Living conduits can't help but soak in some of the substance that is flowing through them. Therefore, if we choose to be conduits of love, the love flowing through us will change us in powerful ways. The opposite is also true. If we are conduits of hatred, resentment, bitterness, unforgiveness, and rage, we will absorb and be changed by these substances, too. Love will bring us life; the latter substances will sap us of what strength and vitality we have left, and over time will set us up for mental, physical, and relational difficulties and dis-ease.

When I allowed love to flow through me, I was soaking up that love myself. I was bearing up under the weight of the devastating situation. I was believing the best of someone who had let me down in a profound way. I was hopeful about my future and even our marriage. I was enduring without weakening. This is what love pouring through me as a living conduit was doing in me and to me.

I believe the spiritual traditions got it right: Love *is* the most powerful force in the universe. It's stronger than hate. It's stronger than bitterness. It's stronger than any force you're up against. When you are in the flow of that most powerful force, when it is in you and pouring out of you, you can't help but be changed by it. *The most life-giving thing you can do in the dark is to love.*

Love's Homecoming

Oftentimes, one of the individuals that needs a heavy dose of our love in the dark is our own self. Maybe we've let ourselves down or believe we're responsible for our loss or the mess we're in. Maybe we don't feel worthy of healing from the awful pain we're in, let alone blooming in the dark. Maybe it feels selfish to love ourselves or that we'd somehow dishonor the loss if we focused on loving ourselves. Or perhaps we've never really liked ourselves and, in a twisted sort of way, the suffering we're experiencing feels deserved or at least familiar.

If you're struggling with loving yourself, it's vital that your love come back home. That you extend to yourself the love and kindness that I've encouraged you to extend to others. Your bloom depends upon it. Plants might be able to bloom without love, but humans can't. Love isn't just a powerful fertilizer; it's a vital nutrient. Indeed, learning to love yourself might just be the greatest thing that happens to you in the dark.

How do we love ourselves? I believe it begins with a decision to be our greatest ally and advocate in life. A decision to refuse to hate or criticize or judge ourselves any longer. A drawing of the line in the sand that from here on out, I will love and accept and choose me, no matter what. Even if no one else does. Forever. Period.

It Pays to Be Grateful

A second powerful fertilizer that we can and should use liberally in the dark is gratitude. I think it's easy for the idea of gratitude to sound glib and pop culture-ish these days, so let me take a moment to explain why I think gratitude is so important for our growth and transformation. First, here's what I'm not saying: I'm not suggesting that we should be grateful for the painful thing that got us into the dark. Losing a child or another loved one or being raped or violated or cheated on or diagnosed with a devastating illness or any other trauma you might have suffered is not something we are thankful for, nor is our goal to get to the place where we become thankful for these traumas. I'm also not suggesting that we pretend to be grateful when we're really not feeling that way. Gratitude works when it's authentic, not when it's forced or faked.

What I am suggesting is that we make a choice to actively look for and acknowledge the things that are going well in our lives (or have gone well in the past) while we are in the dark. Being grateful isn't about denying the very real difficulty you have endured. Instead, gratitude is choosing to acknowledge the difficulty *and* choosing to focus on things and people we are thankful for, even if just for a moment. For example, I'm not thankful my marriage ended in divorce. What I am thankful for is the support I received during that time from family, friends, colleagues, and professional healers. I'm thankful for the changes that took place in me. I'm grateful it spurred me on to become a writer and a dancer. And I eventually became thankful for being released from a situation in which I was not happy or loved and now have a second chance to experience these things in my life.

All of us, no matter how dire our situations have become, can find something to be thankful for. The Buddha once said, "*Let us rise up and be thankful, for if we didn't learn a lot today, at least we learned a little, and if we didn't learn a little, at least we didn't get sick, and if we got sick, at least we didn't die; so, let us all be thankful.*" In other words, if you're still breathing, you've still got something to be thankful for. And if you're not thankful today that you're still breathing (because breathing means you're still dealing with this painful situation), I get it. I hope that tomorrow or next week or the week after that you breathing here with us is something you are able to be thankful for. I'm sure thankful you're still here, and I know I'm not the only one.

Maybe your expression of gratitude is something as simple as being thankful that there was hot water for your shower this morning. Or food in the pantry or gas in the car. Maybe it was the smile from the stranger when you crossed the street or the man who let you go ahead of him in line at the grocery store because he could tell you were in a hurry. Life is full of things to be thankful for when we set our minds to see them.

This approach to gratitude is backed by a good deal of scientific evidence. Grateful people are happier, are more optimistic, have better relationships, sleep better, have stronger immune systems, and recover from stress more quickly[42]. Loss may even cause us to become more grateful people. In a study of 350 adults who had lost a parent during childhood, 79 percent said that they became a more grateful person as a result of the loss[43]. Life became more precious to them, and so did their loved ones.

One of the reasons gratitude is a potent fertilizer is because it doesn't take much to experience an effect. In the research studies, when participants wrote down just three things they were grateful for three times a week over the course of two weeks it was enough to experience greater well-being, less distress, better sleep, and a reduction in blood pressure[44]. In other studies, making a gratitude list once a week for ten weeks or daily for two weeks resulted in positive mood, improved physical health, greater optimism, and improved sleep[45].

Another powerful gratitude intervention is the gratitude letter. For this exercise, individuals write a letter to someone that they want to thank for having a positive impact on their life. Someone that they haven't properly thanked yet for their kindness and influence. Ideally, they then hand-deliver the letter to this person and read it to them. Participants who did this reported an immediate increase in happiness that lasted for a month[46].

Listen to what one young woman who lost her father to suicide just two months prior said after taking a writing workshop with me on gratitude:

> *"Some days when I have no energy after a long day at work, even twenty minutes of writing seems daunting. On those days, I at least write my gratitude list. One day, I made a list of joyful moments I was grateful for that have occurred in the last few weeks. This was really beneficial for me—to see on paper that in the midst of this tragedy there were still joyful moments. Because some days it feels like I won't have any again, which I know isn't true. On those days, I can just jot down a few things I am grateful for and remember that life isn't all tragedy and grief."*

How Do Love and Gratitude Work?

When we use the fertilizers of love and gratitude we shift our mental focus, and as we've seen many times in the previous chapters, what we focus on determines our mood, our thoughts, our behaviors, and eventually the direction our life goes in. But love and gratitude aren't just mental states; they're also behaviors. That means they're something that we can actually do. And this is good news because when we're in the dark, it can feel like we're just hanging out in limbo-land waiting for the situation to change or someone else to change or for the grief to lessen. Gratitude and love are ways for us to take positive action in our situations, effecting change and enhancing a sense of control and agency in our lives. They are also a way for us to create a positive emotional state. Purposeful action, a sense of agency, and positive emotional states are critical psychological resources for growing and blooming. Gratitude and love are also synergistic, meaning they influence one another. The more we feel grateful, the more we are inspired to love. The more we love, the more we have to be grateful for and the easier it is to express gratitude.

Your Turn

In the writing exercises below, you will have the chance to practice using the two powerful fertilizers of love and gratitude. You will explore how you can make a daily choice to be a conduit of love, as well as identify and overcome some of the barriers you face when it comes to loving. You will write about what a "love's homecoming" would look like in your life and what it would be like to be your own greatest ally. You will also have the opportunity to express gratitude by creating a gratitude list and writing a gratitude letter. We'll conclude with a creative gratitude activity you might consider doing over the next few months or year. This is a favorite of mine and I think you'll enjoy it, too.

WRITING PROMPTS

The Love Check-Up

Use the following questions to do a love check-up on yourself. This is not meant to foster self-judgment, but rather to provide an honest look at how much you're using your love fertilizer and what might be getting in the way if you're not using it as much as you'd like.

- While you're in the dark, what is the greatest opportunity for you to love?

- How loving do you feel right now? How loving are you behaving?

- What, if anything, is getting in the way of loving?

- How might your situation change if you decided to extend love?

- Do you typically love to get something or love to become something? What's the difference?

Loving Changes the Lover

Have you ever had an experience in your life where loving someone changed you? Or perhaps you've witnessed this happen in someone else's life. What did you experience and/or learn?

In what ways do you want to be changed by love during your time in the dark? How can you use love as a fertilizer for your blooming process?

Being a Living Conduit for Love

Take a few minutes and respond to the following questions:

- What are you a living conduit for? In other words, what is flowing through you on a regular basis (e.g., love, joy, kindness, resentment, bitterness, anger, etc.)? What impact is this having on you?

- What do you think of the idea of being a living conduit for love?

- Why do you think love is the secret ingredient for blooming in the dark?

- What would it look like if you were to become a living conduit for love? How might this remove the pressure and limitations of loving others (and yourself) with your own love?

Love's Homecoming

Do you have trouble loving yourself? Do you struggle with self-judgment or self-criticism? What would it look like if your love "came back home" to you? What would be different in your life if you were your best friend and greatest ally? How would you feel? How would you behave? How would you speak to yourself?

If you are ready, plan a love's homecoming. Write down the specific things you commit to doing from here on out to love yourself with all you've got. What will you do? What will you stop doing? How will you draw the line in the sand and commit to loving yourself completely and forever? Is there anything you need to do before you're ready to make this commitment? What is it and when will you do that?

My Gratitude List

On a blank sheet of paper write the title, "The Things I Am Grateful for." Take a deep breath and write for five minutes about what you are grateful for in your life, what makes you happy, the gifts and blessings you have been given. These can be big things and small things. They can be everyday pleasures, moments of beauty, kindness from others, nature, people in your life, opportunities, experiences, and so on. Be as specific as possible.

Once you are done, read over your list and really savor each item. Then notice how you feel emotionally and physically. Consider posting this list somewhere you will see it often. Be sure to leave room so that you can continue to add to it.

This is an exercise that seems to have the most benefit if you do it regularly, such as a few times a week or once a week over the course of many weeks. Or, you might try writing down one thing for which you are grateful each night before you go to bed for a few weeks.

Thank-You Letter

You are invited to write a personal gratitude letter to an individual of your choice. Pause for a moment and think about someone who did something very kind for you, who helped you in some way, or who did you a big and lasting favor. It might be someone you are close to, someone you met only once, or someone you've never met, but who has had a major influence on your life. It's also okay to write to someone who is no longer living.

Consider the positive impact this person's kindness had on you. Think about how you felt immediately after receiving this person's help. Reliving those moments can provide you with the words to say in the letter. The more detailed and specific you can be in your letter, the better.

Once you are finished writing the letter, you might consider reading the letter out loud to this person or mailing it to him or her. Or read it out loud as if the person were in the room with you. It is also fine to just tuck it away in your own files.

Fertilizing with Love and Gratitude Frequently

Love and gratitude are blooming fertilizers that can and should be used liberally and frequently. It's impossible to use them too much! What will you do to remind yourself to use love and gratitude frequently during your time in the dark?

Heartfelt Moments Jar

> "It is only with the heart that one can see rightly;
> what is essential is invisible to the eye."
>
> —Antoine de Saint-Exupery

The following writing activity is a contribution from my colleague Lolly Forsythe-Chisolm, a Mind/Body Specialist at the University of Maryland, Baltimore. This is an activity that is meant to be practiced over several months to a year to help cultivate a life of gratitude.

Decorate a container with a collage, doodle, or paint (or all three) to collect "heartfelt moments" over the next few months or year. Making the container helps you create positive intentions and serves to inspire you. Throughout the year, on small pieces of paper, write down good things that touched your heart or made you smile, and put them in the jar. This is a way to celebrate good things that happen each week. Add at least one moment to your jar each week.

Materials

- Glass jar, coffee can, oatmeal container, shoe box, gift box or pretty container, flower pot, ready-to-paint container from an art store

- Any combination of decorative items, including:

  Magazines

  Glue

  Paint

  Pens/markers

  Stickers

  Glitter

  Wrapping paper

  Tissue paper

  Ribbon

When you are finished decorating your jar (or buying one, if making one doesn't sound fun to you), write a meaningful word(s), such as a "focus word" for the year (or your blooming word!) or a favorite quote, on the sides or bottom of your jar. These serve as reminders of what you want your focus to be during this time of your life. Each week, choose at least one heartfelt moment you experienced and write it out on colorful paper and place it in your jar.

Heartfelt Moment Examples:

- An achievement

- An event you enjoyed

- A kindness you witnessed

- A kindness you enjoyed doing for a friend/family member/
co-worker

- One good thing that happened to you

- Something that warmed your heart

- Something you were grateful for

- Evidence of your blooming

Writing Exercise: Summing it All Up

After several months or at the end of the year, read each of the things you wrote and placed in your jar. Write about the insights you glean: What do you love? How you want to spend your time? Who is important in your life? What brings you joy? What fills you up? What are you grateful for?

BLOOMING CHECK-IN

1. What came up for you as you completed your writing prompts in this chapter? Did you experience any "aha moments"? If so, what were they?

2. In what ways did you grow this week, even just a little bit? Did you make any changes? What are you proud of?

3. How will you continue to apply this blooming principle in your life?

BLOOMING TIP

Writing about gratitude and love is a powerful way to supercharge our blooming process. That said, we must go beyond writing and also put these virtues into action. I invite you to let your writing be the catalyst for expressing love and gratitude as you go about your day. Make it a goal or a game to become known as someone who loves well or who is really grateful, or both! You might also think about other fertilizers you can use in the dark. Love and gratitude are potent ones, but they're not the only ones. Have you experienced any other "substances" in your "living conduit" that have benefited you and/or others? One that comes to mind is forgiveness. Can you think of others? How could you use these fertilizers as well while you're in the dark?

CHAPTER 9

MINING THE MESS

Every adversity, every failure, every heartache carries with it the seed of a greater or equal benefit.

—Napoleon Hill

A friend recently invited me over to her house for the first time. I was impressed with how clean her home was, particularly since she was looking after her two-year-old niece for the weekend. At one point, we were sitting at her kitchen table, chatting and drinking tea. From that vantage point, I could see through the glass pane on the front of her oven. Inside the oven was a stack of pizza boxes. Noticing my gaze, she sheepishly admitted that she hadn't had time to put the trash out before I arrived and had stuck the empty boxes in the oven, hoping I wouldn't notice. I assured her I didn't care if there were pizza boxes in her oven or on her counter or anywhere else for that matter. Life is messy, and that's before looking after a toddler!

Later, as I thought about those pizza boxes and my friend's flushed face when I noticed them, it got me thinking about how we handle our messes in life. We typically think of a mess as something bad, something we need to clean up, hide, try to forget about, or pretend never happened. We might close the door to a messy bedroom, sweep clutter indiscriminately into a drawer, or shove things we don't know what to do with into the garage or attic. When we invite people over, we take them into the tidiest room, ensuring they stay far away from wherever we've hidden our mess. And if the mess has gotten out of hand, we make up reasons to meet somewhere other than our house.

This kind of strategy can work for physical messes (at least for a while), but it's not such a great strategy for emotional or relational messes. These types of messes tend to follow us around until we've addressed them, no matter how good we think we are at hiding them or pretending they never happened. In this chapter, on the ninth principle of blooming in the dark, I offer you an alternative strategy for dealing with your emotional messes: *Mining the Mess*. This is a phrase I use with my clients to describe the process of looking back at what has happened in our lives to figure out why and how we contributed to the mess in which we have found ourselves. Armed with that precious knowledge, we can make the changes we need to bloom in the dark.

The Gems Are in Your Mess

It's not easy to think about the messes in our lives, and especially not about how we may have contributed to making them. All kinds of emotions can come up when we think about our messes—blame, self-condemnation, self-hatred, shame, guilt, anger, resentment, and fear, to name a few. Some of us avoid thinking about our messes because we think doing so means we will have to clean it up, and that feels like an impossible task. I'm not actually suggesting we need to clean up all of our messes, or that we should even try. Sometimes clean-up is possible, like when we apologize for a mistake and work toward the restoration of a relationship. But there are many times and situations in life that don't allow for cleaning, and trying to clean up these kinds of messes can cause us more harm—for example, trying to repair a friendship with someone who has repeatedly hurt you or who doesn't want to be a part of your life, or trying to convince your boss to "unfire" you or the bank to erase your bankruptcy, or spending your life wishing someone was still in it. There are many losses and messes that simply can't be undone or cleaned up.

Mining your mess is a different approach. Few of us think about the gems hidden in our messes. These valuable jewels are waiting for us in the dark, dirty, damp, and disappointing places of our history. If we will stop avoiding the mess and instead approach it with a sense of curiosity and expectancy, the riches we can glean are unparalleled. You just can't find these kinds of gems in the light when things are going well for you. Your personalized gems, the ones that will propel you into a better future and a better you, are found in your mess.

To Mine, We Must Search for Meaning

The purpose of mining the mess is so that we can learn from our painful experiences and from any mistakes we may have made. This process equips us to do things differently in the future. Many people think they are mining their mess, yet they don't experience any positive changes. In fact, they can end up making themselves downright miserable. I want to distinguish this behavior from the mining I'm suggesting we do in the dark. After experiencing loss and pain, it is normal for us to think about what just happened. In fact, for a period of time, it's hard to think about anything else. Unfortunately, if we just leave it at thinking about the mess, it can lead to unhelpful rumination and blame of self and others. This in turn can make us feel depressed and anxious and leaves us stuck in old patterns.

The difference between thinking about our mess and mining our mess is meaning-making. When we find meaning in our mess, we are mining the lessons that will allow us to change course. When we simply think about the mess, we stay stuck in the past way of doing things. There is a whole field of research on loss and bereavement that has discovered some very helpful things about healing from loss. These researchers have discovered that it is not time that heals all wounds, but rather it is meaning that heals all wounds[47]. Making meaning or making sense of our painful experiences and our potential role in them is what leads to healing and transformation. In other words, reflecting on the mess plus finding meaning and lessons to be learned equals mining the mess.

REFLECTING ON YOUR MESS
+
FINDING MEANING AND LEARNING LESSONS
= Mining the Mess

One of the reasons that writing is such a great tool for blooming in the dark is that it is an effective way for us to mine our mess. We can go beyond ruminating about our pain to discovering the messages and lessons that allow us to move forward on a different path. When we are willing to really look at the pain we have experienced, it can open our eyes to a reality about ourselves, others, and life in general to which we were once ignorant. It gives us the opportunity to change. Mining the mess, then, becomes a way of redeeming the pain.

Would You Like to Take a Mulligan?

It takes humility to see ourselves as we really are, and it takes courage to change when we don't like what we find. What do we do when we find those kinds of "gems"? One of the things we can do is take a mulligan. Let me explain.

In my opinion, mulligans are the best thing about golf, which tells you how well I play golf. A mulligan is a do-over. It means you can take your shot over again without a penalty to your score. In a sense, you get to act as if the first shot you just sent sailing into the woods or that plunked into the pond never happened. It's a second chance. Golfers who play by strict rules usually don't allow mulligans, but those who play recreationally usually have some various understanding about how many you can have during a game and when you can use them.

Wouldn't it be great if we got life mulligans? If we got second chances and our first failed attempt was not held against us? I sure could have used a few mulligans in my marriage. *Sorry, hon, I think I'll take a mulligan on that unkind remark or that selfish action. Let's just pretend it didn't happen, okay?* If only it were that easy. Unfortunately, the harm has been done, and even if we've been forgiven, the hurt isn't forgotten. Depending on how badly we fired off that first shot, many times the damage is not easily repaired.

We may not be given mulligans by our spouses or employers or friends, and we may not be great at granting them either, whether it be to ourselves or someone else. But I believe that the dark offers us the chance to take a mulligan, to start again.

Now, mulligans and second chances aren't that useful if we didn't learn anything from the first shot. If you don't take some time to think about what you did that caused your shot to go off course, you'll most likely end up taking the very same shot with the very same outcome again. Mulligans are only useful if you first learn from your mistake. That's why mining the mess is so important. This is where we learn from our mistakes, so that we're ready to take the mulligan.

Pain Is an Invitation

Pain is an invitation to mine the mess and take a mulligan. Pain gives us the opportunity for a do-over. It communicates that something isn't working. It's a signal that something needs to change, otherwise the pain will continue. We might not get a do-over with the same job or relationship or financial decision. However, if we pay attention to what message the pain is trying to convey, we will learn some valuable information that allows us a do-over in our next job, relationship, financial decision, and so forth.

A couple years ago, I had coffee with a man whose wife had left him several months before. I asked him what he'd do differently next time. I wanted to see if he had mined his mess. I was impressed with his ready reply. He had obviously given some serious thought to what had gone wrong in his marriage and how he had contributed to its failure. He was heartbroken about his wife's decision to leave and was determined not to make the same mistakes again. He looked forward to the day when he would get a marriage mulligan, a fresh start with someone else who would benefit from what he learned from the mistakes in his first marriage.

This was a man who was consciously choosing to become a better version of himself, so that he could be a better husband. His mistakes, and his wife's, cost him deeply. Rather than self-destructing in bitterness, he was choosing to get up, be honest with himself, and put in the effort to go in a new direction. Pain had taught him, he had listened, and he was hopeful about his second chance. It brought me so much pleasure to recently learn that he has married a beautiful, vibrant woman whom he treasures and treats like a queen. She is his mulligan, and given his commitment to his do-over, I'd say they've got many wonderful, loving years ahead of them.

Celebrate Your Mess

Not only do we need to mine our messes, but we also need to celebrate them. In the computer-animated movie *Meet the Robinsons*, Lewis, a twelve-year-old orphan, spends all his time inventing things. Unfortunately, each of his inventions end up in some sort of disaster or big mess, which scares away all of the prospective parents that might have adopted him had it not been for the messes. I won't ruin the movie for you if you haven't seen it, but there is one scene that was especially meaningful for me. In this scene, Lewis is sitting around the dinner table with a family of inventors. His latest invention does what all of his inventions have done—it fails. And so Lewis expects what he has always experienced—rejection and humiliation. Instead, the family starts cheering and celebrating. "You failed! You failed!" they chant joyously, lavishing him with love and acceptance. Why did they make such a big deal of his failure? Because they understood that failure is a necessary ingredient of success. As my coach likes to say, just like falling down is baked into learning to walk, so too is failure baked into learning how to lead a happy and successful life. So, go ahead and celebrate your failures and your messes. They are baked into your blooming process.

Your Turn

At this point in the blooming process, if you have been using this book in sequential order, you will have mined many lessons from your painful life experiences. The writing exercises below will provide you with the opportunity to reflect on what you've learned. You will approach your messes to find meaning, rather than ruminating on them or marinating in self-blame or self-pity. You are invited to put the lessons you glean—your gems—down on paper, freeing your mind to move forward. Remember, it's important to use your writing as a tool to find meaning. In one study, people who merely relived upsetting events through their writing without focusing on finding and creating meaning reported poorer health than those who derived meaning from the writing[48]. You will also be invited to write about what life mulligans you'd like to take and what this would look like. Finally, you will also have the chance to celebrate your messes and failures as a necessary ingredient of your success, well-being, and blooming.

WRITING PROMPTS

Making Meaning out of the Mess

Psychiatrist Victor Frankl, when reflecting on his experiences in a Nazi concentration camp, wrote, *"Man is not destroyed by suffering; he is destroyed by suffering without meaning."* Based on the reflection and writing you have done so far in your blooming in the dark process, how are you now making sense of what happened to you? What meaning have you given to your suffering? What emotions come up when you look at your situation through this lens of meaning?

My Gems: Ten Things I Have Learned in the Dark

It has been said that our fiercest enemies can be our greatest teachers. Make a list of at least ten things you have learned through experiencing this difficult time in your life. These might be things you have learned about yourself, others, relationships, your priorities, your strengths and weaknesses, spirituality, and life in general. Elaborate on how you learned each of these things. Notice what feelings come up for you as you make this list and take some time to write about these emotions.

Using My Gems to Bloom in the Dark

Once we find meaning and the lessons to be learned in our mess, it's important that we act on these messages. What changes have you made in your life as a result of what you have learned? What changes do you still need or want to make based on what you've learned? What are you proud of? What's one thing you want to do differently moving forward? What impact will this change have on your life?

Taking a Life Mulligan

Can you relate to the need for a Life Mulligan? What would this type of mulligan look like for you? What do you need in order to grant yourself this mulligan? How will life be different once you do?

When you're finished journaling, close your eyes and imagine yourself in this fresh, new state. See yourself as this new creation and feel in your body what it will be like to embody this new you. By creating a vivid image, you provide your mind, body, and spirit instructions for the direction in which you desire to go. The more you practice this visioning exercise, the stronger these instructions become and the easier it becomes to move your life in this new direction.

I Failed! Celebrating the Mess

What do you think of the idea that failure is baked into success? How do you view failure and messes in relation to your blooming process?

Have you celebrated your messes and failures? If no, why not? If yes, what was that like?

Take a few minutes to congratulate yourself in writing not only for making a mess, but also for being willing to look at it closely and learn from it. Be your own best cheerleader here. If you're having trouble with this, think of Thomas Edison, the individual who invented the lightbulb. He failed hundreds if not thousands of times before he successfully created the lightbulb. Imagine how discouraging this could have been and how much we would have missed out on if he didn't mine his messes, learn from them, celebrate his failures, and keep on going. With this in mind, consider that you are on the verge of success and every failure has brought you one step closer. Provide yourself with some encouragement and celebration to fuel your fire to keep on blooming.

BLOOMING CHECK-IN

1. What came up for you as you completed your writing prompts in this chapter? Did anything surprise you? Did anything delight you?

2. In what ways did you grow this week, even just a little bit? Did you make any changes? What are you proud of?

3. How will you continue to apply this blooming principle in your life?

BLOOMING TIP

One last important note about mining your mess. Once your mess has been mined, the process stops. There is only so much to be mined, only so many gems to be extracted. Mines can be dangerous places. Don't stay any longer than you need to, but also don't leave until you have extracted every last hidden gem. You're there now; you might as well get the job done. But when you're done, get out of the mine. It's not your home.

Finally, I hope you find yourself like Lewis, surrounded by people who see your goodness and potential and are cheering "You failed!" with as much love and joy and acceptance as they did for him. I'll join my voice with theirs: You failed! Well done. I'm excited to see who you become and what you do next!

Night Bloomer: Steve Jobs

When we think of Steve Jobs, we think of Apple and the brilliant ideas and inventions that have changed the way we interact with one another and with our technology. We don't think about how he dropped out of college after one semester or was fired from the company he co-founded or his failures in business. Instead, we think about his vision, creativity, and passion and the incredible products his company has produced that many of us use on a daily basis. When asked about his remarkable success, Steve credited it to his failures. As with all Night Bloomers, Steve Jobs courageously used his failures and losses to become more than he could have been without them. Below is a snippet from Steve's 2005 commencement speech at Stanford University in which he describes in his own words his failures, the lessons he learned, and the results he achieved by not giving up.

"I had just turned thirty. And then I got fired. How can you get fired from a company you started? ... What had been the focus of my entire adult life was gone, and it was devastating. I really didn't know what to do for a few months. I felt that I had let the previous generation of entrepreneurs down — that I had dropped the baton as it was being passed to me. I was a very public failure, and

I even thought about running away from the valley. But something slowly began to dawn on me — I still loved what I did. The turn of events at Apple had not changed that one bit. I had been rejected, but I was still in love. And so I decided to start over.

"I didn't see it then, but it turned out that getting fired from Apple was the best thing that could have ever happened to me. The heaviness of being successful was replaced by the lightness of being a beginner again, less sure about everything. It freed me to enter one of the most creative periods of my life.

"During the next five years, I started a company named NeXT, another company named Pixar, and fell in love with an amazing woman who would become my wife. … In a remarkable turn of events, Apple bought NeXT, I returned to Apple, and the technology we developed at NeXT is at the heart of Apple's current renaissance. And Laurene and I have a wonderful family together. I'm pretty sure none of this would have happened if I hadn't been fired from Apple. It was awful-tasting medicine, but I guess the patient needed it. Sometimes life hits you in the head with a brick. Don't lose faith." [49]

CHAPTER 10

ACCEPTING AND LETTING GO

It was my letting go that gave me a better hold.
—CHRIS MATAKAS

"What will you gain when you lose?" In 2011, Kellogg's paired its Special K cereal with this thought-provoking question to give women a new perspective on weight loss. Instead of seeing dieting as a painful process of loss and deprivation, they suggested it could be a process of positivity and inspiration. In the advertisements, when women stepped on the scale, instead of seeing a number they might or might not like, they saw words like confidence, joy, and esteem. The idea was that these were the sorts of things they could gain as they lost weight (and, of course, the suggestion was that eating the cereal would help make this happen).

Whatever your thoughts are about dieting or Special K, the question itself is brilliant. As Night Bloomers, I'm asking you the same question: "What will you gain when you lose?"

Perhaps you will gain confidence when you lose your fear. Or you perhaps will gain peace when you lose your focus on grief. Or maybe you'll gain freedom from attachment. Boldness for inhibition. New ways of doing things for rigidity and routine. Acceptance for denial. Assertiveness for anger. Joy for a negative outlook. Self-love for shame. New possibilities for outdated dreams.

We stand to gain so much when we are willing to lose what no longer serves us. And that's what the tenth principle of blooming in the dark—*Accepting and Letting Go*—is all about. In the last chapter, we mined our mess and learned our lessons. Now, it's time to accept the reality of our situations and let go of what we've been holding on to, so that we can move into the new.

It Starts with Acceptance

Just like the weight loss process begins with acceptance of our current weight, so too does blooming require accepting our current life situation. Acceptance. What comes up for you when you hear that word? I imagine you might have a number of reactions. Acceptance might not feel fair or possible or even desired. Maybe you've already been told that you need to accept your situation, and every time someone suggests this it feels insensitive; maybe it even makes you feel angry.

It certainly did for me for a while. I didn't want to accept that my marriage was over. That went against my value system and my heart's desire. Some people would say I didn't have a choice—if he doesn't want to be married to you, you have no choice but to accept the divorce, they'd say. But that's not true. I did have a choice; I still have a choice. I know people who have been divorced for decades who have still not accepted the fact that they are divorced. Not surprisingly, they're miserable a lot of the time.

I had a choice whether or not to accept my situation, and so do you. It's an important choice we must all make at some point in the blooming process. I finally started experiencing true peace of mind when I made that choice, but it took a lot of time and work to get to the place where I was ready to do so. You may or may not be ready to make the choice to accept today. But in the meantime, let's explore what acceptance would mean for you and what would help you get there.

"I Accept" Is Your Secret Weapon

Beyond it being a choice, what is acceptance? Acceptance is allowing things to be exactly as they are, without trying to push away what we don't like or grasp at what we do like. It means looking at the truth of our life and accepting it exactly as it is without trying to fix or change it. When we accept something, we let go of the illusion that things are or will be different. It doesn't mean that we agree with what we are accepting. It just means that we stop fighting against or denying our reality.

Acceptance is a stance that looks squarely at the messes in our lives and says, "I accept." I accept the loss. I accept the grief. I accept that the relationship has ended. I accept the decision I don't agree with. I accept the pink slip. I accept the diagnosis. I accept the foreclosure. I accept the closed door, the slammed door, the burnt-to-the-ground door. I accept that this is where I am, who I am, and what I've got right now.

Now, acceptance doesn't mean that we don't desire or even pursue change. It simply means that change is not possible until the present is accepted as fact. In other words, acceptance comes before change. And a change in our circumstances usually begins with a change in us.

The power and paradox of acceptance is that it often results in the relief and freedom we thought was only possible if we got what we were striving after. Rather than forfeiting control, acceptance can result in a greater sense of control. With those two powerful words—"I accept"— you can end a war you may have been fighting for years. Maybe you have been warring with regret about a decision you made or a relationship you lost. Maybe you're fighting not to accept an illness, disability, or character trait. Or perhaps your war is more external, such as with a challenging person, an unfair job situation, or a financial issue outside of your control. Whatever you are struggling against, the emotional distress from doing so can drain your energy and make your body sick. Acceptance is a way to put down the proverbial rope, to release the tension, stress, and misery and choose to go in another direction. It's a way to be back in the driver's seat of your life again.

Sometimes we even end up with the very thing we just accepted not having. Sort of like the woman who, after trying so hard and for so long to have a baby, stops trying and then suddenly finds herself pregnant. But we can't count on this paradox of acceptance. At times, life works like this, but not always. Sometimes it's a good thing that life doesn't work out this way because the thing we thought we wanted turns out not to be the best thing for us after all. Regardless of whether we obtain what we accept not having, the act of accepting our reality brings inner freedom and peace. That makes acceptance well worth the effort to achieve.

It's Time to Let Go

Acceptance frees us up for the next step: letting go. It can be hard to loosen our grip. We make hanging on mean all kinds of things. We think it means we haven't given up, we're strong, we're living up to our value system, we're not forgetting someone we love, we're showing we care, or we're honoring a memory. But hanging on to something that no longer serves us can actually harm us.

It's spring as I'm writing this chapter. The other evening, I was walking through my neighborhood delighting in the fragrant trees bursting into colorful buds and flowers. I could feel the energy of new life all around me. That is, except for a pair of trees at the end of the street. Their branches were still full of dead, brown leaves. All the other trees had released their leaves last fall, but these two trees had hung on to theirs, almost like they hadn't accepted that the season had changed and it was time to let them go. Like they had decided dead leaves were better than no leaves. Now it's spring and there is no room for their new leaves to grow. They have sabotaged their blooming season by staying stuck in the past. These trees are a beacon not of new life, but of what happens when we are afraid to accept and let go.

Forgiveness

There are lots of ways of letting go. Let's look at three of those ways here. One way to let go is to forgive. Like acceptance, forgiveness can be a loaded word. So, first, let's talk about what forgiveness is not. Forgiveness doesn't mean you agree with what happened. It doesn't make what happened justified or right. It doesn't mean you're suddenly going to forget what happened to you. It also doesn't mean you have to reconcile with the person who hurt you or even trust them again.

So, what is forgiveness? Forgiveness involves both accepting and letting go. It is accepting that the past will never be different than it is, and it is a choice to let go of or cancel the debt someone owes us. It's accepting that someone will not or cannot pay a bill they owe us, and so we stamp "paid in full" on their bill instead. It is an act of grace and humility. Mark Twain put it well when he said, "Forgiveness is the fragrance that the violet sheds on the heel that has crushed it."

But forgiveness isn't just about self-sacrifice. It's not just someone else that goes free. Forgiveness is also self-preservation and self-betterment: The most important part of forgiveness is that we are set free. Forgiveness is a powerful way of letting go of negative emotions we have stored inside, such as resentment, anger, bitterness, rage, and self-pity. It's a way of freeing ourselves from a painful past and accepting responsibility for how we will create our present and our future.

We can forgive others or ourselves, and many times we need to do both in the blooming process. We can even forgive God for ways we may perceive that he has let us down. Usually the person we are forgiving doesn't need to know that we've done so, unless he or she has asked for our forgiveness. It can be more hurtful to tell someone we forgive them if they haven't sought out our forgiveness, as we may be the only one who perceives that they have done us wrong. In that case, telling someone that we forgive them can cause more conflict and pain. It only takes one person to achieve forgiveness, and that one person is you.

Active Surrender

A second way of letting go is called active surrender. When we think of surrender, we might think of defeat, as in an army surrendering to its enemy because it knows it cannot win. In this context, surrendering sounds like a last resort, the lesser of two evils, the next-best thing to being annihilated. However, active surrender doesn't have to be a last-resort choice, and it's certainly not about defeat.

It is in our nature to want to be in control of our lives. Because surrender is a releasing of (perceived) control, we find it difficult to do, even when logically we know the things we are surrendering are outside of our control. However, in making a decision to surrender, we are actually taking control by making a choice to end a struggle. It is similar to the paradox of acceptance in that when we release our control—or our illusion of control—we finally achieve a greater sense of control, particularly over our emotional well-being.

It's called "active" surrender because there is nothing passive or easy about this. It takes work to surrender. It takes strength of mind and character to surrender. It takes a lot of trust and hope of a better future up ahead.

The methods of active surrender are varied. Some people surrender through writing in their journal or crafting (but usually not sending) a letter outlining what and why they are surrendering. Others surrender through prayer. This kind of surrender is called active spiritual surrender, in which we relinquish control to God or a higher power. Still others surrender through confiding in a trusted other, such as a good friend or a counselor.

Letting-Go Ceremonies and Rituals

A third way we can let go is by engaging in a symbolic action, such as a ceremony or ritual. This is a formal marking of the decision to let go. It's a way of achieving closure and also momentum toward a new desired future. The action one engages in to memorialize the choice to let go is personal. What works for one person may not be meaningful for the next. In crafting your own letting-go ceremony or ritual, you will want to think about what would be most meaningful to you. Other factors to consider when planning your ritual is where you will perform it; who will be with you, if anyone; and when you will do it.

I had my letting-go ceremony in the Grand Canyon on the last Monday in May of 2014. I realized only later the significance of the day I happened to choose: It was Memorial Day. Here's what I wrote in my journal about that experience:

> I hiked down to the three-mile point on the Bright Angel trail. About thirty feet to the right of the covered rest area, filled with weary hikers grateful for a few minutes in the shade, I noticed a large boulder. I hiked over to it and was surprised to find a ledge about three feet wide between the boulder and the sharp edge of the cliff. Standing on the ledge in front of the boulder, I was completely hidden from the hikers in the rest station. I laid my pack down and as I did I saw a small cactus with three yellow flowers by my feet. They were the only flowers I had seen on the hike. I took it as a good omen.
>
> I unzipped the side pocket of my backpack and took out the wedding picture. With a deep breath, I looked at it one last time. There stood two strangers, arms around one another. I didn't recognize the man in a tux standing beside me. I hadn't seen that man in years. I didn't recognize the smiling bride either. She, too, was a thing of the past. I expected tears, but none came. They had all been shed over the last twelve months.
>
> "Thank you, God, for this marriage and the time we had together. It's yours now." With that I carefully tore the picture down the middle, ripping my husband apart from

me. I looked at my smiling face and said, "You, beautiful woman, are free." Then I ripped both halves of the picture into tiny pieces and held them tightly in one fist as I got down on my knees. I opened my hand slightly and gazed at the shards. I saw not only my marriage, but also my fear of being alone, my belief that I was unlovable and unwanted, my refusal to see that I had had an unhappy marriage, my efforts to win my husband back, and my belief that I had failed because I was getting a divorce. What I didn't know when I started this blooming process was that the outcome would be so much bigger and more important than the survival of my marriage.

The paper shards felt heavy then, like a handful of sharp rocks. "Forgive me for littering in the Canyon," I whispered with a brief flash of a social conscience, and then I opened my hands over the side of the cliff and released the weighty shards. I peered over the edge of the Canyon and watched the pieces flutter downward until they were out of sight.

As I was getting back on my feet, I heard what sounded like echoing whoops of victory. Startled, I looked around trying to find the source. Somewhere below me, it sounded like several people in a rock cavern were whooping and hollering with childlike abandon, the rocks echoing their delight. It continued for several more seconds and then stopped. It was the only time during my exploration of the Canyon I heard sounds like these. It was as if the angels themselves were rejoicing as I finally let my marriage go for good.

Now, of course, you don't need to go to the Grand Canyon to let go, and your ceremony may have a different emotional overtone than mine. You might feel a sense of mourning rather than rejoicing or perhaps a mix of emotions, some of which may be unexpected. The ceremony you create and the emotions you feel will be unique to you and your situation. Typically, the common elements of a letting-go ceremony are honoring what was, acknowledging that it is now over, releasing it willingly, and making space for what will be.

Your Turn

Now it is your turn to explore what you will gain when you lose—when you accept and let go of what no longer serves you. The following writing prompts will help you do just that. You will have the opportunity to explore things in your life that you may be resisting accepting. You'll write about what it would be like if you were given permission to look at your "mess" and to simply say "I accept." This has been a powerful exercise in my clinical practice, and I think you'll find it to be the same for you. You'll also be encouraged to write about what you're holding on to and whether or not you like the reasons why you're holding on, as well as what might help you loosen your grip. Finally, you'll have a chance to use the three methods of letting go we discussed above: forgiveness, active surrender, and planning and engaging in a letting-go ceremony or ritual.

WRITING PROMPTS

Taking Stock

To get started, write down whatever comes to mind when you read these two sentence stems:

1. I am able to accept that …

2. I have difficulty accepting that …

Saying OK to the Mess

Sometimes the very best thing we can do with the situations we can't control in our lives is to accept them and stop trying to make them be any different than they are. Internally, we turn and face the mess in our life, drop our weapons, nod our head, and say "I accept." When you cease and desist, the war has to end. Write about the messes in your life that you want to stop fighting to change. What would it be like to look at those messes and simply say "I accept" to them? Try writing your cease-and-desist speech to each mess. Then write about how you feel as you accept and surrender your attempts to deny, change, or fix the messes.

Loosening Your Grip

Spend some time answering the following questions:

- What are you holding on to and why?

- What have you been loosening your grip on?

- What else do you want to loosen your grip on?

- Through your blooming process, what is loosening its grip on you?

Write Your Own "Special K" Message

Just like Kellogg's advertisements displayed what people could gain when they lost weight, write your own "Special K" message by answering the following question: What will you gain when you lose? Notice what thoughts and emotions come up as you write about this. Explore those in your writing, too.

Forgiving Others

A powerful tool for letting go is forgiveness. Is there someone in your life that you hold a grudge against? Someone you resent, dislike, hate, or even wish harm to? This may be someone who is in your life now, someone from your past, or even someone who is no longer living. This could also be God or a higher power.

Rather than writing about the injustice itself, take this time to try to get into the shoes of the perpetrator. Write about why this person might have done what he or she did. Do you know anything about the circumstances of his or her life or childhood that might help to explain the hurtful action?

Then, write about what it would be like to forgive this person—to release him or her (and yourself) from the hope for a different past and from the debt this person owes you. If you are ready, you can even write a statement or declaration of forgiveness. Remember, in doing so you are not saying that what happened was okay. Rather, you are choosing to give up the negative emotions that are hurting you, asserting your power and freedom, and taking charge of your present and future. And remember: It probably isn't a good idea to send your message to that person.

Forgiving Yourself

Is there anything for which you need to forgive yourself? If so, try writing a letter of forgiveness from your present self to your past self. You might express the following in your letter:

- Your understanding of the difficult situation

- Empathy for the feelings and thoughts you experienced at the time

- Your recognition of the circumstances that made it more likely for you to take the action you did (or that prevented you from taking action)

- Your acceptance of your action (or lack thereof)

- The valuable lessons your current self learned from that experience, including what you would do now (or have done since) when faced with something similar

Active Surrender

Active surrender is another way of letting go. What do the words "active surrender" conjure up for you? In what ways would active surrender benefit you right now? How might doing so cost you?

Next, draw a line down the middle of a page of paper. On one side, list what you are ready to surrender now. Then write about how you would like to go about surrendering these things. On the other side of the paper, list the things you are not yet ready to surrender. Then write about what steps you need to take to work toward active surrender.

What I'm ready to surrender now	What I'm not ready to surrender yet

My Letting-Go Ceremony or Ritual

If you are ready, plan and then carry out a letting-go ceremony or ritual. The common elements of a letting-go ceremony are honoring what was, acknowledging that it is now over, releasing it willingly, and making space for what will be.

In planning this symbolic action, you will want to think about what would be most meaningful to you. Other factors to consider when planning your ritual are where you will perform it; who will be with you, if anyone; when you will do it; and what objects you may need.

After you have performed your ceremony or ritual, write about your experience, including what thoughts and emotions came up for you.

BLOOMING CHECK-IN

1. What came up for you as you completed your writing prompts in this chapter? Do you feel heavier or lighter now? If so, what caused that change?

2. In what ways did you grow this week, even just a little bit? Did you make any changes? What are you proud of?

3. How will you continue to apply this blooming principle in your life?

BLOOMING TIP

Acceptance and letting go may be a process for you, like peeling back the skin of an onion, one thin layer at a time. If this is the case, you may find yourself accepting a situation a little at a time, working your way towards complete acceptance and then working toward letting go. Or, acceptance and letting go may function more like a once-and-for-all decision for you, where one day you make the choice to accept the situation in its totality, like closing a door and throwing away the key. There is no right or wrong way to go about the practice of acceptance and letting go. Writing about what works best for you, and how this approach may change across situations, can shed more light onto how you want to move forward with your current situation.

In addition to the tools above, meditation is another great way to work towards greater acceptance and letting go. Mindfulness meditation—an intentional focus on the present moment without judgment—helps to develop our mental abilities of awareness and acceptance. You might try meditating for five or ten minutes before you sit down to write, and then again for a few minutes after you finish your writing session. It can also be enlightening to journal about what comes up for you during your meditation practice.

Night Bloomer: Kirt

Kirt came to see me four years after his divorce. A reserved forty-two-year-old, Kirt felt an enormous weight of guilt for the failure of his marriage and for jeopardizing the future of his two small boys. He had struggled his whole life to be vulnerable and intimate with other people, and he was dismayed that he had turned out just like his father, repeating familial patterns with his boys. He was sure that if he had been able to open up with his wife, their relationship could have been salvaged. He had spent the last four years in and out of court regarding custody matters, with little to show for it besides a growing debt from lawyer fees. The court experiences infuriated his ex-wife, further eroding his confidence in his ability to communicate his wishes and needs. He couldn't even contemplate sending her an email without days of intense anxiety.

He would tear up when he discussed his children and how he was sure he had ruined their lives by leaving their mother. He didn't see his value as a father, comparing himself to the rubber bumpers in a bowling alley that kids use to prevent gutter balls. Besides preventing them from ending up in the gutter, he didn't know what else he could accomplish in the little time he saw them each week. Work was also a source of stress. He would spend his evenings ruminating and worrying about what he had said or done during the work day, which impaired his sleep and his mood. He was embarrassed about his accent, having been born abroad, and found himself unable to assert himself at work, despite being in a managerial position. He had stopped exercising and wasn't eating a healthy diet. As a result, he had gained twenty pounds and felt poorly about his body.

When he began working with me, he had been in a relationship with another woman for three years. He thought he loved her, but he was fearful of a future with her or anyone else. In his mind, love and marriage meant someone had to sacrifice themselves, someone had to lose. He expressed a sincere desire to experience real intimacy with his children and girlfriend and to break the patterns of his past and his family history. No one but his girlfriend and I knew he was struggling with depression, not even his mother or sister who, at the time, lived in the same house as him. It was another source of shame to him.

After we explored who he wanted to become and processed the grief he felt about the divorce, we began to mine the mess. Kirt realized that before the divorce, he was on the road for work all the time. He spent very little time at home with his wife and boys. As a result of the divorce and the soul-searching it prompted, he changed his work schedule so that he would have more time to see his boys. Although he no longer lived in the same house as them, he realized that he spent far more quality time with his children now than he had before the divorce. Over time, he began to tell his boys that he loved them, words he had never heard from his father. Then he started having more in-depth conversations with them and doing things like turning off the radio in the car so that they could get to know one another better.

After mining the mess, he worked on accepting the fact that he was divorced and was gradually able to let go of the self-blame and condemnation. This freed up some confidence to begin to interact with his girlfriend more intimately and assertively. He started checking in with her every Tuesday night about their relationship—what was going well and what they could do better the next week. Their relationship began to thrive with this new intentionality and openness. From her positive reactions, he learned that he could ask for what he needed and be respected for it. He recently bought a house, and she has moved in. He no longer fears marriage, knowing now that it can be a win-win situation.

He began exercising and eating a healthy diet and shed the post-divorce weight. His body image has improved considerably, as has his energy. In the last few months, he has gone on several vacations with his girlfriend and friends, something he used to dread. Now, he finds himself opening up and having real, meaningful conversations with the people in his life. Instead of feeling ashamed about his accent, he volunteered to direct the diversity committee at work, where he now advocates for people who may think that they have less of a voice. Instead of spending his evenings ruminating, he now blogs about his life and what he's learning.

I knew we had reached the final stage of blooming in the dark when he sent me a recent blog post in which he had written about his struggle with depression and anxiety—a piece that he then shared with his friends and the entire family, essentially "outing" himself and his struggles for the first time. He said he wanted to help others who were in the dark, to let them know that they were not alone and that there was help and hope. And just today, he sent me his latest blog, entitled, "A couple things I learnt from my divorce that may save your marriage!" Kirt didn't just come full circle; Kirt bloomed in the dark.

CHAPTER 11

WAITING AND WATERING

The journey is part of the experience—an expression of the seriousness of one's intent. One doesn't take a train to Mecca.

—ANTHONY BOURDAIN

As we are nearing the end of the twelve blooming principles, I imagine that some of you may be wondering where your bloom is. You might feel like you are behind schedule or that things aren't happening fast enough. I get it. I think waiting is the hardest part about blooming. Waiting can feel like a whole lot of nothing, and if you're not doing anything, how could you possibly reach your goal?

Yet, this way of thinking will get you into trouble. You see, how you approach your waiting period—which has everything to do with your mindset about waiting—is of crucial importance in the blooming process. The ancient Taoist practice of wei-wu-wei is helpful here. Wei-wu-wei means doing without doing or action through inaction. Sometimes doing nothing, or focusing on what is happening internally rather than externally, is the most productive thing we can do.

In the Introduction, I described how the metaphor of this book came to me. My friend texted me a picture of the bright pink flower on her night blooming cactus. She said she had been watering it for *years* and that it finally bloomed the previous night. Although the actual bloom appeared overnight, it took a long time before the plant was

137

ready for this seminal moment. Your blooming process might not take years (although if it does, that's okay, too!), but it will take time. Usually more time than we'd like.

When we look at nature or agriculture, most of the time between planting a seed and harvesting the fully-grown crop is spent waiting. That's why the eleventh principle of blooming in the dark is *Waiting and Watering*. This chapter will help you to develop your patience and perseverance, so that you don't give up before your bloom is ready. We'll look at the purpose and rewards of waiting, and the courage and mindset it takes to persevere.

Patience: Two Marshmallows Are Better than One

I've always been a two-marshmallow girl. That's just my nature. That is, until it comes to pain and suffering, and then most days I'd be content with one marshmallow. Let me explain. In the 1970s, Dr. Walter Mischel and Dr. Ebbe Ebbesen, psychologists at Stanford University, set out to understand why some children, but not others, are able to put off immediate gratification if it means they will get a larger reward later. They designed a study to help figure this out called the Stanford Marshmallow Experiment (think of the parents' bragging rights to say that their child was invited to eat marshmallows at Stanford!).

The children in the study, aged three to five, were seated at a table in a room by themselves. The experimenter placed a marshmallow, a cookie, or a pretzel, depending on what the child preferred, on the table in front of the child. She was told that she could eat the marshmallow now, but that if she waited she could have two marshmallows later. Then the experimenter would leave the room and wait about fifteen minutes, an eternity to the poor child who had nothing to do but sit and look at the fluffy lump of goodness in front of her.

It must have been hilarious to watch them. The researchers reported that some of the children would turn their backs to the treat, kick the table, lick the marshmallow, or even stroke it like a little pet, all in an attempt to resist the temptation to eat the marshmallow. Some didn't even try to resist and ate the marshmallow as soon as the experimenter left the room. Only one-third of the children were able to resist eating the treat long enough to be rewarded with two treats[50].

Interestingly, later studies using this same research paradigm found that the children who could delay gratification were more successful in life. Years later, they had higher grades, went farther in school, and were at a healthier weight. It was thought that the more self-control, not to mention patience, discipline, and perseverance, a child had, the longer they could delay gratification[51]. These same traits are necessary to achieve good grades, attain an advanced degree, and maintain a healthy body weight. They are also necessary for blooming.

Emotional Pain Makes Us Vulnerable

As an adult, most of us would have no problem waiting fifteen minutes to eat a marshmallow. This wouldn't be much of a temptation—unless we hadn't eaten for a day. At that point, even if you don't like marshmallows, that one sitting in front of you would seem awfully appealing. Isn't that true with other things in life? When we are hungry or tired or stressed, it can be a lot harder to wait. Vulnerability has a way of short-circuiting our best intentions.

That's why it's critical, when we're in the middle of desperate life circumstances, that we do two things. First, we remind ourselves how vulnerable we are. And second, we get clear about why we are waiting and what we're waiting for. When we are vulnerable, we do not make good decisions. Alcoholics Anonymous uses the acronym HALT to help its participants identify when they are most vulnerable to slipping and having a drink. HALT stands for hungry, angry, lonely, or tired. When we are in those physical or emotional states, we are less likely to exhibit self-control and more likely to give into temptation.

When you are in emotional pain, you are in an almost constant state of vulnerability. That state of loss craves to be satiated—immediately—

and if you can't have the thing that you lost you may find yourself going after replacements. Ever wonder why the first relationship after a breakup has its own special name: the rebound relationship? It's because we often jump into the next relationship too quickly as a way of soothing the pain. Pain relievers do not make good long-term replacements: not for people, jobs, or dreams.

If you've just sustained a major loss, you're not in a good position to make important decisions right now. That can be a frustrating realization. Not only are you suffering, but now you are faced with the fact that making a decision to relieve that suffering may end up prolonging or even exacerbating the suffering. Sitting with pain is not easy. It takes work to be patient with your circumstances and with yourself. In the long run, however, it can save you much time and heartache from having to deal with the messes we create when we try to rush the healing process.

The Purpose and Rewards of Waiting

There is a purpose for your patience. You are not just waiting for the sake of waiting. You are waiting for at least one of two important reasons. You are waiting because there is something you want, or you are waiting because the very process of waiting is transforming you. Let's look at these two reasons more closely.

1. *You are waiting because there is something that you want.*

The first reason you may be in a season of waiting is because there is something that you want. If you are going through a divorce or have lost an important relationship, then you are likely yearning for love and companionship. You don't want to be alone, and sometimes it feels like any old person will do. Some days you'd willingly take back the person you lost, even though you know that relationship wasn't healthy for you. I remember posting the following quote as a reminder to myself to wait for a loving relationship, not just someone to fill the hole in my heart: "*Don't give up what you want most for what you want now.*"

What do you want most? Is that different from what you want now or what you'd be willing to settle for right now? Take a moment right now to put this book down and think about what it is that you really want. If you want a reminder, go back and read your responses to the blooming intentions prompts in Chapter 1.

Not having our immediate needs met for a period of time can be a gift because it gives us the opportunity to think about what we *really* want. When you know what you really want, you will be much less likely to settle for what you think will stop the pain right now. You will be able to remind yourself that what might feel good right now likely won't feel that good later, especially if it means you sold your chance to have even more. My sister drove this point home one day when I told her I had gone on a date with a man who, although he didn't have one of the key attributes I was looking for, treated me well and said wonderful things about me. She said, "I'm glad you had a good date. I am supporting you in finding your Big Love." Big love. Yes, that is what I really wanted. I appreciated the reminder that there are lots of nice guys out there, but I wasn't after a nice guy. I was after Big Love and this was my chance to have that.

This is your chance, too. I know it probably doesn't feel like much of a chance. Loss feels miserable, and we all want to get out of misery as fast as possible. This is when you have to tell yourself that the emptiness you feel is not going to destroy you. You are capable of holding that emptiness rather than filling it with the first thing that comes along. Explore that emptiness and see what would fill it best. Then wait for that thing or that experience or that person. You are waiting for a reason. You want two marshmallows, not just one. This is your chance to wait for your heart's true desire. Remember, we will always be settling if we make decisions out of desperation. You will be giving up something important if you go after temporary pain relievers when you are in the middle of your suffering.

2. *You are waiting because waiting is transforming you.*

Sometimes what we need most is the inner transformation that can only be achieved through patience. That is, the waiting itself is changing us and causing us to bloom. I don't think we are here on Earth to have a problem-free, happy life, although there is nothing wrong with being happy. I like being happy as much as the next person. However, ultimately, I believe we are here to learn, grow, and love. I also believe we are each here to complete a special, personalized mission and that we are equipped to fulfill this mission through the living of our life. The equipping and the completing of our missions are processes that require much patience.

More often than not, what you are waiting for, what you want, is not as important as the transformation happening inside of you *as you are waiting*. There are so many phenomena in the natural world that show us that beautiful things happen when we are willing to be patient in our trials. Take the pearl, for example, which grows inside the belly of an oyster. The happy, pain-free oysters never grow pearls. They live a much less stressful life, but the end result is so much less glorious than that of the oysters who were subjected to an unending trial.

When a foreign substance enters the shell of an oyster, such as a grain of sand, the oyster goes to work to protect itself from this irritating substance. It covers this foreign substance with the same material that is used to make its shell. It puts on layer after patient layer of this material and eventually a pearl is formed. Did you notice that the irritant, the stressor, the source of pain, is never removed from the oyster? If it were to be removed, the very precious reward for its struggle is lost. It is in growing with and through the stressor, not the removal of the stressor, that the pearl is formed. The longer the oyster must contend with the irritant, the larger the pearl will grow. That means that the most costly pearls in the world came from the oysters that suffered the most and for the longest.

If you find yourself waiting, remember that there is a good purpose for this. You may be waiting for something you really want or you may be waiting because the waiting itself is causing inner transformation. My guess is that it's some of both. Don't cheat yourself by short-circuiting the process.

It Takes Courage to Persevere

As I mentioned earlier, ironically, I'm not a big gardener. I do have a thing about weeds, though. I may only have shrubs and dirt in my front garden, but that doesn't mean I tolerate the dandelions that think the unoccupied dirt is an invitation to take up residence. I pluck up those dandelions fast.

One day when I was walking up to my house, I noticed a familiar yellow fuzz by the front steps. I bent over to pluck it up and then stopped. This dandelion was different. It hadn't chosen to grow in the rich soil of the "flower" garden or even within the expanse of grass that covered the front lawn. No, this dandelion had chosen to grow in the middle of the *pavement.* One of the concrete slabs leading up to the front porch has a slight crack on one side. This dandelion had chosen to grow up right through that small crack in the concrete. How it found enough dirt or even enough sunlight to grow in that tiny dark place I will never know. But it had, and here it was in full bloom in the middle of my sidewalk.

I didn't pluck that dandelion. I figured if it had worked that hard to bloom in the inhospitable concrete then it deserved to live out its days there. For the next week and a half, whenever I'd walk up to my house, I'd pause for a moment to look at that dandelion. It impressed me.

That little flower taught me an important lesson about perseverance: It takes courage to grow in tough places. It takes courage to bloom. The fact that you are still here reading this book, determined to bloom, impresses me. I know that to be interested in reading a book like this whatever you are going through is tough. You might be just trying to survive long enough to get to the other side of your situation. Some of you need to know that there is another side. I understand. Some days all I could do was hang on. I didn't think I had the energy to grow, and some days I didn't have the desire either.

I can look back on those days now and realize that choosing to persevere when I would rather have given up, choosing to get up and go to work when I'd rather have spent the day in bed, choosing to counsel my clients in the clinic when I'd rather have fallen apart myself—those were all choices to grow. Those choices stretched me. They caused me to become more than I was. I learned how to give even when I felt empty. I learned how to encourage someone else when I needed encouragement myself. I learned how to put others first when all I could think about and all I wanted to talk about was myself and my own pain. These might sound like small steps, but they were big for me, and they required courage. Becoming more other-focused was one of the ways I grew as a result of the pain. It wasn't easy, but growing in tough places never is. It requires perseverance and courage.

You May Be Closer than You Think

When we're in the middle of a trial, the end can seem a long way off. You may have been in this so long that you have stopped believing there is an end to it. I remember a backpacking trip I did in the Rocky Mountains in Alberta, Canada, the summer before my eighteenth birthday. It was just me, a woman about twenty years older than me, and our guide. We hiked for miles and miles each day with a heavy pack. If I had known the trip was going to be that intense, I would have spent more time training for it. I remember one day in particular. We had hiked for about seven miles in the July heat, my feet were sore, and my shoulders had deep grooves from the weight of my pack. Our guide signaled that we were going to stop for a few minutes to rest, as we had reached the halfway point in our hike for the day. He had found a little lake off the trail and we gladly heaved our packs to the ground and stretched out on the grass. I closed my eyes and felt my body sink into the ground. The sun was warm on my skin, the breeze was light and cool. It remains one of the most extraordinary moments of relaxation I've ever had.

After about ten minutes, I thought to myself, okay, I'm ready, I can do this. Seven miles down, seven to go. I strapped my heavy pack back on and we trudged toward the trail. In half an hour I saw an opening in the trail, a stream, and some other hikers setting up camp. I figured we'd fill up our water bottles and keep on moving. The last thing I expected to hear was, "We're here!" I know I looked confused. We still had a good six miles to go. That's when my guide smirked and said he had been kidding when he said we were at the halfway point. We were really just around the corner. I actually felt disappointed because I had mentally prepared for several more hours of hiking and here we were finished for the day. As soon as he said we had arrived, my body became weary and I felt like resting. I realized through that experience how critical our mindset is for facing challenges. When I had prepared for more arduous hiking, my body felt up for the challenge. When I was told it was time to rest, my body felt like doing nothing but resting.

Your mindset is critical, especially now. You may be closer than you think. Remember, the night blooming cactus suddenly bloomed one night. It's good to prepare for as long a journey as it takes, but also to remember that your destination could be right around the corner. As you engage in the work of blooming, I encourage you to look for and fully enjoy the moments of rest and joy. These moments of seeming inactivity are inwardly recharging you for whatever lies ahead. You have been working hard, and you have everything you need to bloom. You might have some more waiting and watering to do, but if you'll keep at it, your appointed time for blooming will surely come.

Your Turn

The following writing prompts will help you move with greater ease through this stage of waiting and watering. You will have a chance to assess the progress you have made and how you're feeling about this progress. Then, you'll have the opportunity to develop your patience muscles by considering the practice of wei-wu-wei and how this practice could help you during this stage of blooming. You'll also dive into the purpose of your waiting period, as well as the unique reasons and rewards for your waiting. Finally, you'll have the opportunity to shore up your perseverance by considering courageous actions, tweaking your blooming mindset, and writing an encouraging letter to yourself for days when you need some extra cheerleading.

WRITING PROMPTS

Assessing My Progress

Take a few minutes to check in with yourself. How far along are you in your blooming process? Did you think you'd have made this much change already? Or, are you feeling the opposite in that you were hoping you would have made more change by now? There is no right or wrong answer. Just write about where you're at, as well as the feelings that are coming up as you check in with yourself.

Practice Wei-Wu-Wei

Wei-wu-wei is an ancient Taoist practice of action through inaction that can help us during periods of waiting. What would "doing without doing" or "action through inaction" look like for you right now? How could this practice or mindset help you in your blooming process? What emotions come up as you consider these ideas?

Two Marshmallows Are Better than One

In the classic psychology study, children who waited to eat a marshmallow were rewarded with two marshmallows. What is your "one marshmallow"? What are your "two marshmallows"? In other words, what is it that you *really* want, versus what you want or could have right now? In what ways are you vulnerable to settling for one marshmallow? What can you do to reduce your vulnerability and ensure that you wait for your two marshmallows?

Waiting on Purpose

What is the purpose behind your waiting? Are you waiting because there is something that you want? Or, are you waiting because the process of waiting is transforming you? Or is it some of both? What meaning can you derive from this period of waiting for your bloom?

An Encouraging Letter from My Hero

Think about one of your heroes or role models. This might be someone you know well or someone you have never met, but whom you have read about or seen on TV. For this exercise, you will write as if you are your hero who is writing you an encouraging letter. What would this person say about where you're at in your blooming process? What would he or she say to help inspire your patience and perseverance? What advice would he or she have for you? Address the letter to yourself and sign it from your hero. Reread your letter on days that you need some extra encouragement.

Courage to Persevere

Can you relate to the story of the dandelion growing up through the crack in the pavement? If yes, how so? If no, is there another story of perseverance that you can relate to better? What courageous choices—choices to stretch and grow—do you need to make to continue to persevere and bloom? What would help you to make those choices?

Tweaking Your Mindset

What is your current mindset toward blooming? Are you prepared to see this process through until the very end? Are you feeling weary or like giving up? What do you need to ensure that you don't give up too early?

What would it be like if you knew that your bloom was right around the corner? How would your mindset change? What emotions would you be feeling? How would you be behaving? Once you're done answering the questions above, write about how you could begin to live from this place of expectancy.

BLOOMING CHECK-IN

1. What came up for you as you completed your writing prompts in this chapter? What do you want to do with this information about yourself and your blooming process?

2. In what ways did you grow this week, even just a little bit? Did you make any changes? What are you proud of?

3. How will you continue to apply this blooming principle in your life?

BLOOMING TIP

If you're feeling like you're never going to bloom, know that you're not the first to feel that desired change is impossible. Nelson Mandela, a man who led his country into a freedom that was once only the thing of dreams, said, "*It always seems impossible until it's done.*" The people who have seen their dreams come true are the ones who refused to give up.

That said, and this will sound ironic given the topic of this chapter, maybe you do need to give up. Well, not officially give up, but more like hit the pause button for a moment, like I did at the "midpoint" of the hike in Alberta. You might choose to hit pause on blooming for a few hours or for a day or two. Just enough time to recharge and recommit to the process. During this pause, I would highly encourage you to seek out support from your community. Let them know you need some encouragement. Ask them what changes they have seen in you so far. Allow them to cheerlead you. We all have times where we need to be watered by others during this process. If you're feeling on track, then there is no need to take a pause. Keep on waiting and watering.

No matter where you're at right now, remember, Night Bloomers bloom. That's what we're made to do. Your bloom is coming. Stay the course.

CHAPTER 12

CELEBRATING AND SHARING THE HARVEST

The world breaks everyone and afterward many are strong at the broken places.

—ERNEST HEMINGWAY

He was only eleven the first time. They were told the tumor in his brain was inoperable. A second opinion resulted in a shunt to drain the fluid, followed by two more surgeries and months of physical therapy and radiation. The tumor began to shrink and by high school, five years later, the family celebrated the news that the tumor was gone. A once active and athletic boy, Zach was never quite the same, but he kept a positive attitude, made the most of his abilities by managing athletic teams in school, and shared his story with various groups to inspire them that they too could beat cancer.

He was in his first year of college the second time. The surgeon was able to remove about 85% of the new brain tumor. Shortly after awakening from surgery, against his parents' admonishments, Zach lifted himself up in bed, made a muscle pose by flexing his biceps and asked his dad to take a picture. Zach then posted his hospital muscle pose on social media to encourage others that not only was he strong enough to beat cancer a second time, but so were they. Ten thousand people responded to his post and in support sent pictures of themselves making the pose, which had been affectionately named

Zaching. These symbols of strength, courage, and hope inspired Zach to start a foundation in 2013 called Zaching Against Cancer, a nonprofit foundation that provides assistance to people with cancer and their families. The foundation has already provided millions of dollars of support for patients, such as paying hospital bills, providing transportation, cutting lawns, organizing beauty days, offering scholarships, and funding research.

Zach passed away in March of 2014, yet his foundation continues to thrive. Here's what his father said when I spoke with him: "Do I resonate with blooming in the dark? Absolutely. I could have curled up and died or divorced, which so many people do after losing a child. Instead, Zach made sure the very opposite happened. Of course I'm still sad, but every day I celebrate Zach and his mission rather than spend my day mourning. I think Zach had a plan for us all along. He taught us so much. He made our whole family stronger. I never would have experienced this change without this dark time. Zach always lived like this, but it took me going through this tragedy to learn that life is short and we need to live in the moment and enjoy everything. He also taught me the importance of giving back to others. Zach did this for other children with cancer. Now, my wife and I carry on his mission. Every day, because of him and how he lived his life, I get to have a positive impact on the world. It is very special."

Before Zach died, his father, John Lederer, asked him where the muscle pose came from. "Dad, don't you remember?" Zach asked with a smile. His father shook his head, confused. "After my first surgery, when I was eleven, as I was waking up from the coma, you were standing at the end of my bed. You made the muscle pose and told me to be strong. And, so I was."

And, so they both were. Blooming inspires blooming.

In the last eleven chapters, we have examined principles regarding what we need to do in order to bloom in the dark. In this final chapter, we will switch gears. The twelfth principle is about two important actions we need to take once we've reached a state of blooming: *Celebrating and Sharing the Harvest.* In this chapter, we will celebrate where you've come from and who you've become. You will also explore how you can share the fruit of your bloom with others to inspire their blooming. When you find the benefits and blessings and becomings from being in the dark, your suffering story becomes a blooming story. But this isn't the end of your story—this is your new beginning. We'll look at how to use your blooming harvest to continue to create the self, mission, and life you desire. As you keep dreaming big, you set yourself up for more bountiful harvests to enjoy and share with others who also need hope and healing.

Post-Traumatic Growth

While most would never agree to relive the trauma or loss they endured, like Zach's father, many report a growth and strengthening that would not have been possible without experiencing that pain and suffering. The people they become and the impact they have on the world is not in spite of the negative event; it's *because of* the negative event. This is the dark cloud's proverbial silver lining. With time and perspective, many look back on their struggles as unexpected and certainly un-chosen blessings.

In the field of psychology, we call this post-traumatic growth or trauma-induced growth. This concept refers to the positive changes we can experience as a result of struggling with highly challenging life circumstances. These positive changes might occur in an individual's outlook, priorities, life satisfaction, relationships, and spirituality. Indeed, people who are able to find the silver lining in negative life events generally report less negative affect, milder distress, fewer disruptive thoughts, and greater meaning in life. Objective measures also show that they enjoy better physical and mental health, too[52].

We have been working toward this notion of trauma-induced growth by engaging in the blooming process. You might already have seen positive shifts inside and outside of yourself despite the desperate challenges you have faced or are facing right now. Or, maybe you're not quite there yet. As we discussed in the last chapter, whatever you are experiencing is okay. Blooming is a process. Go ahead and read this chapter anyway to support your expectation and to prepare yourself for the blooming that is to come.

Celebrate Your Bloom

When you do reach a state of blooming, there are two important steps to take. The first is to celebrate your bloom. Too often we set a goal, work hard to achieve it, obtain that goal, and then immediately start working toward the next goal. When we operate in this manner, we fail to honor both the outcome and the hard work we exerted to achieve it. Over time, we can lose our motivation to grow and even begin to burn out.

In an earlier chapter, we discussed celebrating our failures. Now, it's time to celebrate our successes and achievements, as well as our effort, perseverance, and courage. This is why we've done the hard work of blooming, after all. This is our reward! To eat and enjoy the fruit of our labor. There are so many things to celebrate—our new way of being in the world, refined character traits, new possibilities and opportunities, the ways we have expanded, how our dreams and goals have changed, and so much more.

Think about where you were when you started this blooming process. Then, think about where you are and, most importantly, *who* you are now. I liken this reflection process to the before-and-after pictures of someone who underwent a makeover. The after picture is always nice, but the real impact is in seeing the contrast between the before and the after pictures. The tangible change between the two is what impresses and inspires.

One of the ways we create this contrast is by re-narrating our stories. In Chapter 2, you wrote your pain and suffering story— the loss or trauma you went through and how this impacted you. Now, it's time to re-narrate your pain story such that it becomes a blooming or redemptive story. We do this by actively searching for the benefits and blessings that occurred as a result of the painful life experience. We celebrate not the event that led us into the blooming process, but the benefits and blessings and positive changes that have resulted from it.

Another way to celebrate your bloom is by having a blooming celebration to mark the end of the old and the beginning of the new. This celebration honors the work you have done and the outcomes you have achieved. This might be a public celebration with friends or loved ones, such as a party or small gathering. Or, it might be a private celebration in which you do something meaningful to you, such as an activity you enjoy or traveling to a place you've always wanted to visit. Or, you might write yourself a congratulatory card or buy yourself a nice gift to mark this important occasion.

Sharing Your Harvest

The second important step to take once you've bloomed is to share your blooming harvest with others. At the beginning of this book, we talked about how important it is not to waste our sorrows. I believe it's equally important not to waste our blooming harvest. One of the beautiful things about blooming is that the fruit you reap far exceeds what you need for yourself.

Think about what happens when a farmer plants a seed. From one carefully planted and nurtured seed comes a plant that produces fruit, and that fruit is home to hundreds of seeds—hundreds of potential plants that will bear more fruit. Take, for example, a tomato seed. From that one seed come dozens of tomatoes, and within each tomato are dozens more seeds that will produce more tomato plants that will bear more tomatoes, and so it goes. The potential for harvest is exponential.

The same is true of Night Bloomers. The outcome of your blooming is abundant and it is meant for so much more than just yourself. You are now well positioned to help others bloom. There is fruit to share and enjoy and seeds to plant for future harvest. For many people, their particular blooming process—their pain that turns to purpose—becomes one of their missions in life. Just like helping people with cancer became one of John and his wife's mission after their son Zach was diagnosed with cancer. Or Nelson Mandela, who used his pain and imprisonment to bring an end to racial segregation and discrimination for millions of people. Or Jenny, who, after her newborn had to be hospitalized and undergo many surgeries, created Hosts for Humanity to provide low- or no-cost housing for families with a loved one in the hospital. Or Kirt, who suffered in secret for years from depression after his divorce and now blogs about mental health issues to help others who are suffering emotionally. Or Renée, who after her own transformation through cancer is helping others who are going through the same process. Or Darcy and Kimberlie, who used their own experiences with trauma to help others heal from their traumatic experiences.

I'm not saying you have to go start an organization or charitable foundation or necessarily do anything formally related to the loss you endured. That may not be your particular mission. What I am saying is that there are and will be people in your life that will need the fruit of your bloom. How will you share your fruit? Who can you support like those who supported you? When we give to others, we plant our seeds for future harvests. There are so many potential Night Bloomers out there. How will you help them bloom?

Your Turn

In this final set of writing prompts, you will have the opportunity to celebrate your bloom and share your harvest with others. You'll create your own before-and-after blooming picture by re-narrating your pain and suffering story into a blooming story. You will also be encouraged to plan and execute a blooming celebration that is meaningful to you. Then, you will have the chance to reflect on how you want to share your blooming harvest with others. You'll write about how your bloom can inspire others to bloom. Finally, you'll continue to be intentional about your life and future by writing about who you want to be and what you want your life to look like twelve months from now. I encourage you to dream big!

WRITING PROMPTS

Silver Linings

Most of us would not willingly choose the pain and suffering we endured. Yet, most of us are also able to find silver linings to our black clouds in life. The following prompts are designed to help you find your silver linings. Use one or more of them to get you started.

- From this hard time in my life I've learned that ...

- My greatest personal strengths are ...

- I'm proud of myself that ...

- I'm amazed that I have been able to ...

- One of the best things to come from all of this is ...

- The way I can now help others is ...

Celebrating Your Bloom

You did it! You bloomed in the dark! It's time to celebrate your achievements, as well as your effort, perseverance, and courage. Use this space to list all the things you have to celebrate. Include all of the blessings, benefits, and becomings as a result of blooming in the dark. You might reflect on the following questions as you write your celebration list:

- What character traits have you developed or refined?

- What is now possible for you because you have bloomed?

- What new doors have opened?

- What can you now say yes to?

- How has your life expanded?

- What gifts has this time allowed you to give?

- What have you learned?

- How have your priorities changed?

- How have your dreams and goals for the future changed?

- How are you different in your relationships?

- How are you different in your own skin?

Also, reread each of your responses to the prompts in Chapter 1 where you set your intention to bloom. Write about how many of your intentions were realized and how much your process resembled the blooming story you wrote for yourself. Finally, write about what still remains to be done or to be bloomed.

My Blooming Story

It's time to re-narrate your pain and suffering story such that it becomes a blooming story. Begin by rereading your story of suffering in Chapter 2. Then, write about where and who you were when you started this blooming process. Next, write about where you are now, and, most importantly, who you are now. Be sure to include the benefits, blessings, and positive changes that have occurred as a result of this painful life experience. Finally, write about the differences you see between the two stories—between your before and after story. What surprises you? What delights you? What are you celebrating most?

My Blooming Celebration

Plan your ideal celebration to mark the end of the old and the beginning of the new. This celebration will honor all the hard work you have done and the amazing outcomes you have achieved. This might be a public celebration or party or a private activity. The important thing is that it is meaningful to you.

Sharing Your Blooming Harvest

You are now equipped to help others to bloom. Some do this in a formal way, such as starting an organization or charitable foundation. Others fulfill their mission and share their harvest in more informal ways, such as by being a supportive presence in the lives of others going through challenging situations. Reflect on how you would like to share your harvest by responding to the following prompts:

- Who are the people in your life that need the fruit of your bloom?

- How will you share your harvest? Do you want to do this in a formal or informal way?

- What purpose has come from your pain? Do you have a new or refined life mission? If so, what is it?

- How will you plant your seeds for future harvests?

- How will you help your fellow Night Bloomers?

Setting Yourself Up for Future Harvests

You can use the same principles you used to bloom, such as setting an intention, taking courageous action, and exerting patience and perseverance, to continue to shape your future and set yourself up for future harvests. Write about who you want to be and what you want your life to look like one year from now. Rather than writing about where you expect to be, write about where you really want to be in all aspects of your life.

Date the top of your page one year from now. Write a detailed description of yourself in the <u>present tense</u> (e.g., I am, I have, etc.). Describe how you look, how you feel, what your mood is, your self-talk, your intentions, your relationships, your work, how you are spending your time, and so on. Be as detailed as possible. Then put your description in a sealed envelope dated one year from now. Open the letter on that specified date and see how much of the future you wrote yourself into!

My Bucket List

A bucket list is a list of all the things you want to accomplish or do before you die. They can be big things or small things. The important thing is that each is something meaningful to you. Creating and then completing your bucket list is one way to reach the end of your life with no regrets and a heart full of beautiful memories.

Once you have written your bucket list, explore a few or all of your items in more detail. For instance, you can write about what interest, value, skill, or strength of yours relates to each bucket list item. What is most important to you about each item?

Review your bucket list often to remind yourself of what you consider the most important ways to spend your precious time and energy. Then take purposeful action to complete the things on your list.

BLOOMING CHECK-IN

1. What came up for you as you completed your writing prompts in this chapter? Where do you notice celebration in your body? What amplifies this feeling?

2. In what ways did you grow this week, even just a little bit? Did you make any changes? What are you proud of?

3. How will you continue to apply this blooming principle in your life?

4. Have you completed your blooming process, or do you have a sense there is more blooming ahead of you? If the latter, what principles and writing prompts might be helpful to revisit?

5. Who in your life might benefit from hearing your blooming story?

BLOOMING TIP

Blooming is an ongoing process and there are always more things to learn, more growth to be experienced, and more harvests to reap. Just as you have been intentional about blooming, I encourage you to be intentional about creating your future and who you want to be in that future. Writing is one way to facilitate this process, just as you have been doing throughout your blooming process. We use our words to plant the seeds from our harvest to create more growth and future harvests. So, keep on writing!

The one thing we can count on in life is change. Tuck these prompts and your responses away somewhere safe, and the next time life presents an unexpected challenge or difficult loss, revisit what you wrote. What wisdom can you glean from what you went through already? What else is there to learn? How else can you grow and bloom?

CONCLUSION

The wound is the place where the Light enters you.

—RUMI

Congratulations, Night Bloomer! I'm so proud of you for courageously working your way through the twelve blooming principles. You chose to look at your suffering from a new perspective: Instead of asking, "Why me?" you began to ask yourself, "Who do I want to become as a result of this suffering and what do I want my life to look like going forward?" You set a strong intention to bloom. You did the hard work of grieving before growing. You found your support system. You were willing to be in the uncertainty of the dark. You expanded courageously. You kept your mind on blooming and fed your hope. You wrestled with the Gardener. You fertilized your bloom with love and gratitude. You mined your mess. You accepted and let go of what no longer served you. You waited and you watered instead of giving up. And then you celebrated your bloom and planned how to share your harvest. Transformation is not easy and you hung in there until the very end. I hope you are exceptionally delighted with the treasures you gathered—the treasure you became—in the dark.

I want to leave you with a few parting thoughts inspired from conversations I've had with my clients and my own experiences in the dark. As you know, most plants don't just bloom once. They have a lifetime of growing and blossoming. Life is cyclical that way. I hope you never, ever have to go through this particular painful situation or anything like it again. That said, life involves loss—big ones and small ones—and no matter how much work we do on ourselves, we can't avoid experiencing loss, or the pain it entails. We can, however, work to become more resilient in the face of loss, which you have done by working through these blooming principles. As a result of your discipline, determination, and courage, you will never face loss the same way again because you are not the same person you were when you first experienced loss. You have resources and resiliency you didn't have before. You have wisdom and tenacity. And you have a blooming under your belt.

It may have taken years for my friend's cactus to bloom, but once it did, she knew without a doubt that that plant could bloom. Now she can expect future blooms. We know the same about you. You're a Night Bloomer. You bloomed, and if you need to, you'll bloom again. Because that's what Night Bloomers do.

Beauty and Brokenness

The other important thing to acknowledge is that even as you are celebrating your bloom and sharing your harvest, you may still experience times of grief and pain. Hopefully not all the time and not at the same intensity. But just because you bloomed, it doesn't mean that you will never feel the pain of your loss again. Life is never the same after a loss. There is beauty for sure, as your bloom demonstrates. But there are also scars that attest to the pain you endured. The following story, called *The Cracked Pot*, gave me hope as I contemplated both the beauty and the leftover ache in my own blooming process.

(The author of this story is, at present, anonymous. One version of the story is found at https://www.moralstories.org/the-cracked-pot/.)

> A water bearer in India had two large pots, each hung on each end of a pole, which he carried across his neck. One of the pots had a crack in it, and while the other pot

was perfect and always delivered a full portion of water, at the end of the long walk from the stream to the master's house, the cracked pot arrived only half full.

For a full two years this went on daily, with the bearer delivering only one and a half pots full of water to his master's house. Of course, the perfect pot was proud of its accomplishments, perfect to the end for which it was made. But the poor cracked pot was ashamed of its own imperfection, and miserable that it was able to accomplish only half of what it had been made to do. After two years of what it perceived to be a bitter failure, it spoke to the water bearer one day by the stream.

"I am ashamed of myself, and I want to apologize to you."

"Why?" asked the bearer. "What are you ashamed of?"

"I have been able, for these past two years, to deliver only half my load because this crack in my side causes water to leak out all the way back to your master's house. Because of my flaws, you have to do all this work, and you don't get the full value from your efforts," the pot said.

The water bearer felt sorry for the old cracked pot, and in his compassion he said, "As we return to the master's house, I want you to notice the beautiful flowers along the path."

Indeed, as they went up the hill, the old cracked pot took notice of the sun warming the beautiful wild flowers on the side of the path, and this cheered it some. But at the end of the trail, it still felt bad because it had leaked out half its load, and so again it apologized to the bearer for its failure.

The bearer said to the pot, "Did you notice that there were flowers only on your side of the path, but not on the other pot's side? That's because I have always known about your flaw, and I took advantage of it. I planted flower seeds on your side of the path, and every day while we walk back from the stream, you've watered them. For two years I have been able to pick these beautiful flowers to decorate my master's table. Without you being just the way you are, he would not have this beauty to grace his house."

As this story so compellingly demonstrates, there is beauty and purpose in the imperfection. The pot's greatest gift was not found in its perfect appearance or its ability to do the job it thought most important. Instead, the pot's greatest service was found in—was because of—its brokenness and willingness to be of service in the state it was in. Hundreds of flowers bloomed *because of* the crack.

You will never forget what you lost, nor should you. It cost you something to bloom. That pain, that suffering, that loss, it caused a crack, maybe a large one, maybe one that nearly split you in two. But that crack is what lets the light in and the beauty out. The crack is how we share our harvest. Indeed, the crack is why there is a harvest to enjoy and share in the first place. As Night Bloomers, we are both broken and beautiful, and we are invited to celebrate both truths. What sets us apart is that our brokenness is redeemed into purpose. And that purpose changes you and it changes your world.

The dark is a fertile place, and beautiful things happen there. You are one of those beautiful things. My parting wish for you is that the treasures you gather in the dark exceed your wildest dreams and that your blooming inspires other Night Bloomers with the courage and hope to do the same.

ACKNOWLEDGMENTS

Of all the things I've had the privilege of doing in my life, there are few things I'm prouder of than the publishing of this book. Probably because I had to live it before I could write it—and the living was much harder than the writing! Knowing that these ideas and tools will help others to bloom in the dark feels like redemption of some very challenging times in my life.

Writing a book and blooming in the dark take a team—a whole garden of support—and I'd like to say thank you to all those who helped me to do both. I am grateful to my writing coach, Laura Oliver, who played a critical role in getting me started on this path by inspiring me to write my memoir. Thank you for the wisdom and loving encouragement you provided during such a vulnerable time in my life. Thank you to my agent, Joelle Delbourgo, for believing in me and this book and for working diligently to find a beautiful home for it. I am grateful for my editor, Fiona Hallowell, and the team at Ixia Press/ Dover Publications. Working with you all has been a delight.

My blooming has so much to do with the support of my family, friends, colleagues, and healers. There are too many to name you all, but I want to say a special thanks to a few: Lea Marshall, your encouraging texts and e-mails kept my head above the water and my heart hopeful during my separation process. Your text about the night-blooming cactus sparked this whole idea. Linda Teague—Heart Mom, I couldn't have chosen a better person to walk through this process with me. Your love and friendship were some of the best gems I was given in the dark. Steve Osterhout, your counsel was just what I needed and I'll never forget your kind and wise words. Wendy Kumar, you have worked your "magic" on me for seven years and helped me through some very challenging times. Thank you for your support, skill, and kind spirit. Krystin Locantore, you were a godsend not just for my hair but also for my heart. I appreciate your friendship, laughs, and counsel. Maggie Reyes, you are truly a top 1-percent coach. Thank you for seeing me and helping me to do the same. To my colleagues, it is such a joy to work *with* you and *for* you. Flav Lilly, your support and assistance continue to amaze me. Thank you for everything. To all my sweet friends, I am beyond lucky to have you in my life. I love you all. To my brave clients who model courage, perseverance, and determination to bloom, you are an inspiration to me. It is such a privilege to work with you.

My dear family, although you live farther away than I wish, you make your love and support known in countless ways and I am grateful. Dad, I quite literally could not have bloomed or written this book without you. You're everything a girl could ever ask for in a father— and more. I'll never forget all the ways you've loved me and taught me I'm valuable (remember the Coke branding talk?) and instilled in me a belief that I can do anything I set my mind to.

To my Divine Gardener, thank you for revealing yourself to me in the dark in such powerful, ever-present, and loving ways. For every shard, a bloom. May my life and this book be a sweet offering to you.

How to Start Your Own Blooming Group

What is a "blooming group"?

A blooming group is like a book group, but its purpose and function differ in important ways. Unlike a regular book group, the purpose is not so much to discuss the book, the author, or literary choices and devices; its purpose is to advance the blooming process of each individual member. It does so by using the principles and writing prompts provided in *Night Bloomers: 12 Principles for Thriving in Adversity*. Group members discuss how they are applying these principles in their lives and what they are learning from engaging with the writing prompts.

A blooming group also differs from a typical support group or grief group in that the focus is less on the darkness and more on the blooming. It's not that you won't discuss the various losses, life upheavals, and tragedies that brought you to the group. It's just that this won't be the main thing you discuss. Those discussions are best for individual or group therapy or a night out with friends. The intention of the blooming group is to forward the blooming process. Since our lives go in the direction of our attention, the group's attention needs to be on blooming. The principles in *Night Bloomers* provide the framework for the group discussions, as well as tools for moving through adversity (rather than just talking about adversity, so we don't get stuck there!).

Why is a blooming group helpful?

We weren't meant to bloom alone. In fact, Principle #3 is all about *Supporting Your Bloom*. A blooming group is one way to do just that. Surrounding yourself with other Night Bloomers who have set the intention to bloom in the dark is very motivating. It's also reassuring to know that you're not the only Night Bloomer out there—sometimes it can be hard to see each other when you're in the darkness of your own loss and grief. Not only does a blooming group help you to build your "garden of support," but it also provides you with the opportunity to be a support for others during their difficult time. The research shows us that helping others is one of the best ways to improve our emotional well-being.

Who can attend a blooming group?

Blooming groups are for Night Bloomers! That means you need to have experienced something in your life that has created "the dark" for you. That might be the loss of a loved one, an illness, being laid off, bankruptcy, trauma, divorce, or another type of stress or adversity. But to join a blooming group, you need to have done more than experience an adversity—you also have to want to bloom in the dark! Maybe that goes without saying, but it's important that even if group members aren't sure blooming is possible for them, there is at least a desire to find out.

Facilitators of the groups will need to use discernment when deciding whether to create a group composed of just one gender or one type of loss or a group restricted to a certain age range. There are pros and cons to narrowing membership. Some people will feel most comfortable in a more homogeneous group and the discussion will necessarily be narrowed to certain themes. However, people often benefit from the diversity of perspectives and life experiences found in more heterogeneous groups.

How many people can be in a group?

A blooming group can be as small as two Night Bloomers, but I would suggest a minimum of three to four members. Although having two members makes for a very intimate group and reduces the challenges that can arise with scheduling for a larger group, groups of this size can be a little more unstable. If one person is absent or decides to stop participating, the group ceases to exist. Although you can technically have as many members as you like, my suggestion is to limit the group to about eight to ten people. Any more than that makes individual participation more challenging. Shy members have a harder time speaking up in very large groups, and it can be difficult to stay within the time parameters while having everyone share. In my opinion, the ideal group size is around four to six members. This size allows for ample individual participation, but it is also not threatened by the occasional absence of a member or two.

How often should we meet?

I recommend meeting twice a month. Weekly meetings are certainly not discouraged, if members would like to meet that often. My experience is that despite enthusiasm, people are busy and often can't commit to meeting on a weekly basis. Every other week is usually doable.

Once a month isn't as ideal as twice a month, as it can be harder to form an intimate and supportive group when that much time goes by between meetings. And if someone misses a meeting, they have to wait two months to participate again.

If it is not possible for members to meet in person twice a month, groups can consider having one face-to-face meeting per month and one online group per month. There are lots of free video conferencing platforms available for these purposes, such as Zoom or Skype.

How long are the meetings?

I recommend groups meet for an hour and a half each time they come together. A group of two members may not need this long and a group of ten might want to extend to two hours. Regardless of the size of the group, I would suggest not going beyond two hours. Delving into these deep and emotional issues can be tiring emotionally and physically (blooming is hard work!). Limiting the group to an hour and a half or two hours helps keep the space supportive rather than draining.

The total length of time, from the formation to the conclusion of the group, can be a little challenging to determine. Some groups might like to commit to a one-year process, where they discuss one blooming principle per month. This works nicely, as there are twelve principles. Others might feel intimidated by the idea of making a one-year commitment and might rather create a six-month group. Still others might find one year not long enough.

My suggestion is to commit to one year, meeting twice a month. The group can always decide to extend after the year is complete, and members that can't continue for whatever reason are free to stop whenever they choose. I found a year to be a realistic timeframe for my own blooming process—not too short and not too long. Most of us need at least a year of good, solid support to get through our blooming process, and a twelve-month group helps to ensure we'll have that.

What is the structure of a blooming group?

I will provide some suggestions for the group structure, but I want to preface these suggestions by saying the group exists for you and the structure should reflect what works best for you. Remember, the purpose of the group is to support the blooming process of the individual members. That means whatever structure best supports your blooming process is the best structure for your group. If you find a structure that works better for you than what I suggest below, I'd love to hear about it!

My suggestion is to meet twice a month for a year. In the first meeting of the month, the group discusses one of the twelve blooming principles: what it means to each member, how it applies to their lives, any questions members might have about the principle or any of the prompts suggested for that principle, and so on. For example, in Month One you'd discuss the first blooming principle, in Month Two you'd discuss the second blooming principle, and so on. Any remaining time in the first meeting of the month can be devoted to discussing what is coming up for you as you are completing the writing prompts (see ideas for the second meeting of the month).

The second meeting of the month is devoted to discussing what's coming up for each of you as you complete the writing prompts and blooming activities—in other words, what insights, ideas, surprises, growth, setbacks, and questions are surfacing as a result of your writing and blooming. You can also each share some of your answers to the blooming check-in questions at the end of each chapter. Although you will be discussing your writing, I recommend not reading your written responses during the group. This can be time consuming and not an effective way to use the time and support of the group. Rather, use this meeting time to discuss what's coming up for you, what you're learning, what themes and patterns you're noticing, how you're applying the material, and how you're blooming.

It's important to note that some members will need to spend longer than one month on certain principles, while others may find themselves moving through the material more quickly. The only wrong way to go through *Night Bloomers* is to go through it at someone else's pace! The goal is for each member to bloom, not for each member to adhere to a specific schedule.

The suggested structure above allows for members to proceed through the material in *Night Bloomers* at different paces. Regardless of where a member is at, the first group of the month can still cover the blooming principle of the month. In this way, all twelve principles will be introduced over the course of a year. The discussion that follows the introduction of the principle in the first meeting of the month and the discussion in the second meeting of the month can be about any of the principles or any of the writing prompts. Members don't need to be at the same place in the book or in their blooming process to benefit from the discussion, support, and insights shared by other members. Group facilitators can emphasize this at the beginning of the group, and periodically throughout the process.

How do I find people to form a blooming group?

The only requirement for joining a blooming group is identifying as a Night Bloomer and wanting to bloom in the dark. So, to start a blooming group, you need to find other Night Bloomers. This means finding others who have gone through or are currently going through some sort of life upheaval, stressor, or adversity and who want to be part of a group that will support them in thriving during their difficult time. To find others who would be interested in this opportunity, you can try a number of different strategies. I'll suggest a few, but feel free to come up with your own ideas, too. And if you find an idea that works well, let me know!

* You can ask your friends if they'd like to be part of a blooming group or if they know anyone in their social circle who might benefit. All of us know at least one person who is going through a tough time, and usually more than one.

* You could give a friend or two you think might benefit from the group a copy of *Night Bloomers* and suggest starting a group together.

* You can post a notice on Facebook or your other social media accounts letting friends know about your desire to start a group. You could also ask them to reshare your post on their accounts.

* You can ask to make or post an announcement in other groups and organizations you belong to, such as a faith organization, a community group, a mom's group, your gym, or your yoga class.

* If you are in therapy, you can ask your therapist if he or she might be interested in facilitating a group, or if you could leave a notice in the waiting room for other clients to see and contact you as the group facilitator.

* If you aren't in therapy, you can reach out to local clinical practices and ask the therapists the same questions listed above.

* You can start a group using the website Meetup.com, which is a great way to meet other local people with similar interests. There are lots of other groups on Meetup.com, such as divorce support groups and grief groups. A blooming group in your area would be a great addition.

You are welcome to use any of the language in this Blooming Group Guide in your posts, announcements, and marketing materials.

Can new members join after the group has started?

The answer to this question will be up to your individual group. Some groups prefer to be "closed," in that they do not accept new members after they begin. Other groups prefer to be "open," meaning new members can join at any time or at set times throughout the duration of the group. There are pros and cons to both ways of doing things. It is best to talk through these preferences with your members when the group is first forming, to create a sense of safety and transparency in how the group will operate.

Who should facilitate the group?

Again, there are a few ways to do this. You can have one facilitator or two co-facilitators who oversee the group logistics and help to get the conversation going or get back on track during the group meetings. Usually the facilitator is someone who has a passion for starting the group and is motivated to see it through to the end. Another option is to alternate who facilitates the group each week, so that each member has a turn at leading the group. In this case, there is still usually a point person who oversees logistics, such as scheduling, sending reminders, finding a place to meet (unless it rotates based on the facilitator of the week), and generally overseeing the functioning of the group.

Are there guidelines the group should keep in mind?

There are a few guidelines I share at the beginning of every group I run. I find doing so helps make the group a safe place and sets expectations for how members show up from the get-go. The first is confidentiality. In order to create a safe and supportive environment within the group, I ask everyone to keep all information shared by other members in strict confidence. They are welcome to share their own experience with others, but they are asked to keep what others share to themselves.

The second guideline is mutual respect. To ensure that members feel comfortable sharing their genuine thoughts and feelings within the group, all members are asked to treat one another with courtesy, respect, and dignity. Treating others with kindness and compassion promotes well-being for the whole group.

The third is the "I pass" rule. While members are encouraged to participate in group discussions, at no time should anyone be asked to reveal information that he or she is uncomfortable sharing. By saying "I pass," the group member's wish to be silent at that time will be honored.

The very first group meeting is a good time to share these guidelines, as well as to solicit other ideas for guidelines from your group. By having some sort of informal acknowledgment, such as everyone raising their hand to show agreement, the group establishes its own set of norms and expectations for participation.

Is there a fee for being in the group?

No! Blooming groups should be free to all members. The only cost involved is purchasing the *Night Bloomers* book, so that members can be doing their blooming work and writing exercises between meetings.

Where should we meet?

There are lots of possibilities for meeting places. You might meet in the facilitator's home each time or rotate so that you meet at some or all of the members' homes throughout the year. You could also meet in a church or another place of worship, a private room at a local library or community center, or a quiet coffee shop. The main requirement for your space is that it is quiet and relatively private. You will be sharing sensitive and emotional things with one another. You want a space that feels safe, secure, and confidential. A place where you won't be disturbed and where you won't be disturbing others.

What resources do we need?

The resources needed are minimal. Each member should bring their copy of *Night Bloomers*, their blooming journal, and a pen. Someone might also want to bring some Kleenex. And cookies.

I would love to hear about your blooming group! You can reach me at www.DrMichellePearce.com and on Instagram at bloomwithdrmichelle. If you post on your Instagram account about your group, please be sure to use the hashtag #NightBloomers and tag me, too. Let's create a blooming revolution together!

NOTES

1. Holland, J.A., and R.A. Neimeyer. 2010. "An examination of stage theory of grief among individuals bereaved of natural and violent causes: A meaning-oriented contribution." *Omega* 61(2):103–20.

2. Pennebaker, J.W., and S.K. Beall. 1986. "Confronting a traumatic event: Toward an understanding of inhibition and disease." *Journal of Abnormal Psychology* 95:274.

3. Pennebaker, J.W. *Opening up: the healing power of expressing emotions.* New York: Guilford Press, 1997. Frattaroli, J. 2006. "Experimental disclosure and its moderators: A meta-analysis." *Psychological Bulletin* 132:823.

4. Bower, J.E., M.E. Kemeny, S.E. Taylor, and J.L. Fahey. 2003. "Finding positive meaning and its association with natural killer cell cytotoxicity among participants in a bereavement-related disclosure intervention." *Annals of Behavioral Medicine* 25:146.

5. Laurent, C. 2003. "Wounds heal more quickly if patients are relieved of stress: A review of research by Susanne Scott and colleagues from King's College. London. Presented at the annual conference of the British Psychological Society." *BMJ* 327:522.

6. Norman, S., Lumley, M., Dooley, J., & Diamond, M. (2004). "For whom does it work? Moderators of the effects of written emotional disclosure in women with chronic pelvic pain." *Psychosomatic Medicine, 66,* 174–183.

7. Harvey, A., & Farrell, C. (2003). "The efficacy of a Pennebaker-like writing intervention for poor sleepers." *Behavioral Sleep Medicine*, 1, 115–124.

8. Smyth, J., Hockemeyer, J., & Tulloch, H. (2008). "Expressive writing and post-traumatic stress disorder: effects on trauma symptoms, mood states, and cortisol reactivity." *British Journal of Health Psychology*, 13(1), 85–93.

9. Davidson, K., Schwartz, A., Sheffield, D., McCord, R., Lepore, S., & Gerin, W. (2002). "Expressive writing and blood pressure." In S. J. Lepore, & J. M. Smyth (Eds.), *The writing cure: How expressive writing promotes health and emotional well-being* (17–30). Washington, DC: American Psychological Association.

10. Park, C., and C. Blumberg. 2002. "Disclosing trauma through writing: Testing the meaning-making hypothesis." *Cognitive Therapy & Research* 26(5):597–617.

11. Poon, A., and S. Danoff-Burg. 2011. "Mindfulness as a moderator in expressive writing." *Journal of Clinical Psychology* 67(9):881–95.

12. Sloan, D., Feinstein, B., & Marx, B. (2009). "The durability of beneficial health effects associated with expressive writing." *Anxiety, Stress, and Coping, 1* (1–15). Suhr, M., Risch, A., & Wilz, G. (2017). "Maintaining mental health through positive writing: effects of a resource diary on depression and emotional regulation." *Journal of Clinical Psychology*, 73(12), 1586–1598.

13. Graf, M., Gaudiano, B., & Geller, P. (2008). "Written emotional disclosure: A controlled study of the benefits of expressive writing homework in outpatient psychotherapy." *Psychotherapy Research*, 18, 389–399.

14. Meston, C., Tierney, A., Lorenz, M., & Stephenson, M. (2013). "Effects of expressive writing on sexual dysfunction, depression, and PTSD in women with a history of childhood sexual abuse: results from a randomized clinical trial." *International Society for Sexual Medicine*, 10, 2177–2189. Schoutrop, M., Lange, A., Hanewalk, G., Davidovich, U., & Salomon, H. (2002). "Structured writing and processing major stressful events: A controlled trial." *Psychotherapy and Psychosomatics*, 71, 151–157.

15. Klein, K., and A. Boals. 2001. "Expressive writing can increase working memory capacity." *Journal of Experimental Psychology: General*, 130(3):520–33.

16. Ramirez, G., and S.L. Beilock. 2011. "Writing about testing worries boosts exam performance in the classroom." *Science* 331:211–3. Spera, E.D., J.W. Buhrfeind, and J.W. Pennebaker. 1994. "Expressive writing and coping with job loss." *Academy of Management Journal* 37:722–33.

17. Smyth, J. M. (1998). "Written emotional expression: effect sizes, outcome types, and moderating variables." *Journal of Consulting Clinical Psychology*, 66(1), 174–184.

18. Zhou, X., X. Wu, F. Fu, and Y. An. 2015. "Core belief challenge and rumination as predictors of PTSD and PTG among adolescent survivors of the Wenchuan earthquake." *Psychological Trauma: Theory, Research, Practice, and Policy* 7(4):391–7. https://doi-org.proxy-hs.researchport. umd.edu/10.1037/tra0000031.

19. Cann, A., L.G. Calhoun, R.G. Tedeschi, and D.T. Solomon. 2010. "Posttraumatic growth and depreciation as independent experiences and predictors of well-being." *Journal of Loss and Trauma* 15:151–66. http:// dx.doi.org/10.1080/15325020903375826.

20. Bourassa, K.J., A. Manvelian, A. Boals, M.R. Mehl, and D.A. Sbarra. 2017. "Tell me a story: The creation of narrative as a mechanism of psychological recovery following marital separation." *Journal of Social & Clinical Psychology* 36(5):359–79.

21. Pennebaker and Beall, 1986. Nolen-Hoeksema, S. "Ruminative coping and adjustment to bereavement." In *Handbook of Bereavement Research: Consequences, Coping, and Care.* Washington, DC: American Psychological Association, 2001.

22. Kross, E., & Ayduk, O. (2011). "Making meaning out of negative experiences by self-distancing." *Current Directions in Psychological Science*, 20(3), 187–191.

23. Smyth, 1998. "Written emotional expression."

24. Pennebaker, J.W. 2010. "Expressive writing in a clinical setting: A brief practical guide to expressive writing for therapists and counselors." *Independent Practice* 30:23–5.

25. APA, n.d.

26. DHS Risk Lexicon, US Department of Homeland Security. September 2008. http://www.dhs.gov/xlibrary/assets/dhs_risk_lexicon.pdf.

27. Unknown author.

28. Kam-Hansen, S., M. Jakubowski, J.M. Kelley, I. Kirsch, D.C. Hoaglin, T.J. Kaptchuk, and R. Burstein. 2014. "Altered placebo and drug labeling changes the outcome of episodic migraine attacks." *Science Translational Medicine* 6(218):218ra5. https://doi.org/10.1126/scitranslmed.3006175.

29. Stroebe, M., and H. Schut. 1999. "The dual process model of coping with bereavement: Rationale and description." *Death Studies* 23(3):197–224.

30. Neimeyer, R.A. 2000. "Searching for the meaning of meaning: Grief therapy and the process of reconstruction." *Death Studies* 24:541–58.

31. Stroebe and Schut, 1999. "The dual process model."

32. ibid.

33. Neimeyer, 2000. "Searching for the meaning of meaning."

34. Andersson, M., and C. Conley. 2013. "Optimizing the perceived benefits and health outcomes of writing about traumatic life events." *Stress and Health* 29:40–9.

35. Reblin, M., and B. Uchino. 2008. "Social and emotional support and its implication for health." *Current Opinion in Psychiatry* 21:201–5. Reinhardt, J., K. Boerner, and A. Horowitz. 2006. "Good to have but not to use: Differential impact of perceived and received support on well-being." *Journal of Social and Personal Relationships* 23:117–29.

36. Holt-Lunstad, J., T. Smith, M. Baker, T. Harris, and D. Stephenson. 2015. "Loneliness and social isolation as risk factors for mortality: a meta-analytic review." *Perspectives on Psychological Science* 10(2):227–37.

37. Holt-Lunstad, J., T.B. Smith, and J.B. Layton. 2010. "Social relationships and mortality risk: A meta-analytic review." *PLoS Medicine* 7(7):e1000316. doi:10.1371/journal.pmed.1000316.

38. Smith, T., J. Ruiz, and B. Uchino. 2004. "Mental activation of supportive ties, hostility, and cardiovascular reactivity to laboratory stress in young men and women." *Health Psychology* 23:476–85.

39. Lipton, B. *Biology of Belief: Unleashing the Power of Consciousness, Matter & Miracles.* Carlsbad, CA: Hay House, 2016.

40. Pargament, K., and S. Saunders. 2007. "Introduction to the special issue on spirituality and psychotherapy." *Journal of Clinical Psychology* 63(10):903–7.

41. Pargament, K.I., H.G. Koenig, N. Tarakeshwar, and J. Hahn. 2001. "Religious struggle as a predictor of mortality among medically ill elderly patients: A 2-year longitudinal study." *Archives of Internal Medicine* 2001;161(15):1881–5. doi:10.1001/archinte.161.15.1881.

42. Emmons, R. *Thanks!: How Practicing Gratitude Can Make You Happier.* Mariner Books, New York, 2008.

43. Greene, Nathan, and Katie McGovern. 2017. "Gratitude, psychological well-being, and perceptions of posttraumatic growth in adults who lost a parent in childhood." *Death Studies* 41(7):436–46. doi:10.1080/0748118 7.2017.1296505.

44. Jackowska, M., J. Brown, A. Ronaldson, and A. Steptoe. 2016. "The impact of a brief gratitude intervention on subjective well-being, biology and sleep." *Journal of Health Psychology* 21(10):2207–17.

45. Emmons, R.A., and M.E. McCullough. 2003. "Counting blessings versus burdens: An experimental investigation of gratitude and subjective well-being in daily life." *Journal of Personality and Social Psychology* 84(2):377–89.

46. Seligman, M. E. P., Steen, T. A., Park, N., & Peterson, C. (2005). "Positive Psychology Progress: Empirical Validation of Interventions." *American Psychologist, 60*(5), 410–421.

47. Holland and Neimeyer, 2010. "An examination of stage theory of grief."

48. Murray, B. 2002. "Writing to heal." American Psychological Association. http://www.apa.org/monitor/jun02/writing.aspx.

49. Jobs, Steve, 2005. Commencement speech, Stanford University. https://news.stanford.edu/news/2005/june15/jobs-061505.html.

50. Mischel, Walter, and Ebbe B. Ebbesen. October 1970. "Attention in delay of gratification." *Journal of Personality and Social Psychology* 16(2):329–37. doi:10.1037/h0029815.

51. Kidd, Celeste, Holly Palmeri, and Richard N. Aslin. 2013. "Rational snacking: Young children's decision-making on the marshmallow task is moderated by beliefs about environmental reliability." *Cognition* 126:109–114. doi:10.1016/j.cognition.2012.08.04.

52. Tedeschi, R.G., and L.G. Calhoun. *Trauma and transformation: Growing in the aftermath of suffering.* Newbury Park, CA: Sage, 1995.

BIBLIOGRAPHY

Addington, E., R. Tedeschi, and L. Calhoun. "A Growth Perspective on Post-traumatic Stress." In *The Wiley Handbook of Positive Clinical Psychology*, 223–31. Madden, Massachusetts: Wiley-Blackwell, 2016.

American Psychological Association. The Road to Resilience, Psychology Help Center, 2019 https://www.apa.org/helpcenter/road-resilience (retrieved December 27, 2019).

Andersson, M., and C. Conley. 2013. "Optimizing the perceived benefits and health outcomes of writing about traumatic life events." *Stress and Health* 29:40–9.

Bourassa, K.J., A. Manvelian, A. Boals, M.R. Mehl, and D.A. Sbarra. 2017. "Tell me a story: The creation of narrative as a mechanism of psychological recovery following marital separation." *Journal of Social & Clinical Psychology* 36(5):359–79.

Bower, J.E., M.E. Kemeny, S.E. Taylor, and J.L. Fahey. 2003. "Finding positive meaning and its association with natural killer cell cytotoxicity among participants in a bereavement-related disclosure intervention." *Annals of Behavioral Medicine* 25:146.

Cann, A., L.G. Calhoun, R.G. Tedeschi, and D.T. Solomon. 2010. "Posttraumatic growth and depreciation as independent experiences and predictors of well-being." *Journal of Loss and Trauma* 15:151–66. http://dx.doi.org/10.1080/15325020903375826.

Davidson, K., Schwartz, A., Sheffield, D., McCord, R., Lepore, S., & Gerin, W. (2002). "Expressive writing and blood pressure." In S. J. Lepore, & J. M. Smyth (Eds.), *The writing cure: How expressive writing promotes health and emotional well-being* (17–30). Washington, DC: American Psychological Association.

DHS Risk Lexicon, US Department of Homeland Security. September 2008. http://www.dhs.gov/xlibrary/assets/dhs_risk_lexicon.pdf.

Emmons, R. *Thanks!: How Practicing Gratitude Can Make You Happier.* Mariner Books, New York, 2008.

Emmons, R.A., and M.E. McCullough. 2003. "Counting blessings versus burdens: An experimental investigation of gratitude and subjective well-being in daily life." *Journal of Personality and Social Psychology* 84(2):377–89.

Frattaroli, J. 2006. "Experimental disclosure and its moderators: A meta-analysis." *Psychological Bulletin* 132:823.

George, N. *The Little Paris Bookshop.* Penguin Random House, New York, 2016.

Graf, M., Gaudiano, B., & Geller, P. (2008). "Written emotional disclosure: A controlled study of the benefits of expressive writing homework in outpatient psychotherapy." *Psychotherapy Research,* 18, 389–399.

Greene, Nathan, and Katie McGovern. 2017. "Gratitude, psychological well-being, and perceptions of posttraumatic growth in adults who lost a parent in childhood." *Death Studies* 41(7):436–46. doi:10.1080/0748118 7.2017.1296505.

Harvey, A., & Farrell, C. (2003). "The efficacy of a Pennebaker-like writing intervention for poor sleepers." *Behavioral Sleep Medicine,* 1, 115-124.

Holland, J.A., and R.A. Neimeyer. 2010. "An examination of stage theory of grief among individuals bereaved of natural and violent causes: A meaning-oriented contribution." *Omega* 61(2):103–20.

Holt-Lunstad, J., T. Smith, M. Baker, T. Harris, and D. Stephenson. 2015. "Loneliness and social isolation as risk factors for mortality: a meta-analytic review." *Perspectives on Psychological Science* 10(2):227–37.

Holt-Lunstad, J., T.B. Smith, and J.B. Layton. 2010. "Social relationships and mortality risk: A meta-analytic review." *PLoS Medicine* 7(7):e1000316. doi:10.1371/journal.pmed.1000316.

Jackowska, M., J. Brown, A. Ronaldson, and A. Steptoe. 2016. "The impact of a brief gratitude intervention on subjective well-being, biology and sleep." *Journal of Health Psychology* 21(10):2207–17.

Kam-Hansen, S., M. Jakubowski, J.M. Kelley, I. Kirsch, D.C. Hoaglin, T.J. Kaptchuk, and R. Burstein. 2014. "Altered placebo and drug labeling changes the outcome of episodic migraine attacks." *Science Translational Medicine* 6(218):218ra5. https://doi.org/10.1126/scitranslmed.3006175.

Kidd, Celeste, Holly Palmeri, and Richard N. Aslin. 2013. "Rational snacking: Young children's decision-making on the marshmallow task is moderated by beliefs about environmental reliability." *Cognition* 126:109–114. doi:10.1016/j.cognition.2012.08.04.

Klein, K., and A. Boals. 2001. "Expressive writing can increase working memory capacity." *Journal of Experimental Psychology: General*, 130(3):520–33.

Kross, E., & Ayduk, O. (2011). "Making meaning out of negative experiences by self-distancing." *Current Directions in Psychological Science*, 20(3), 187–191.

Laurent, C. 2003. "Wounds heal more quickly if patients are relieved of stress: A review of research by Susanne Scott and colleagues from King's College. London. Presented at the annual conference of the British Psychological Society." *BMJ* 327:522.

Lipton, B. *Biology of Belief: Unleashing the Power of Consciousness, Matter & Miracles.* Carlsbad, CA: Hay House, 2016.

Meston, C., Tierney, A., Lorenz, M., & Stephenson, M. (2013). "Effects of expressive writing on sexual dysfunction, depression, and PTSD in women with a history of childhood sexual abuse: results from a randomized clinical trial." *International Society for Sexual Medicine*, 10, 2177–2189.

Mischel, Walter, and Ebbe B. Ebbesen. October 1970. "Attention in delay of gratification." *Journal of Personality and Social Psychology* 16(2):329–37. doi:10.1037/h0029815.

Murray, B. 2002. "Writing to heal." American Psychological Association. http://www.apa.org/monitor/jun02/writing.aspx.

Neimeyer, R.A. 2000. "Searching for the meaning of meaning: Grief therapy and the process of reconstruction." *Death Studies* 24:541–58.

Nolen-Hoeksema, S. "Ruminative coping and adjustment to bereavement." In *Handbook of Bereavement Research: Consequences, Coping, and Care.* Washington, DC: American Psychological Association, 2001.

Norman, S., Lumley, M., Dooley, J., & Diamond, M. (2004). "For whom does it work? Moderators of the effects of written emotional disclosure in women with chronic pelvic pain." *Psychosomatic Medicine, 66,* 174–183.

Pargament, K.I., H.G. Koenig, N. Tarakeshwar, and J. Hahn. 2001. "Religious struggle as a predictor of mortality among medically ill elderly patients: A 2-year longitudinal study." *Archives of Internal Medicine* 2001;161(15): 1881–5. doi:10.1001/archinte.161.15.1881.

Pargament, K., and S. Saunders. 2007. "Introduction to the special issue on spirituality and psychotherapy." *Journal of Clinical Psychology* 63(10):903–7.

Park, C., and C. Blumberg. 2002. "Disclosing trauma through writing: Testing the meaning-making hypothesis." *Cognitive Therapy & Research* 26(5):597–617.

Pennebaker, J.W. *Opening up: the healing power of expressing emotions.* New York: Guilford Press, 1997.

Pennebaker, J.W. 2010. "Expressive writing in a clinical setting: A brief practical guide to expressive writing for therapists and counselors." *Independent Practice* 30:23–5.

Pennebaker, J.W., and S.K. Beall. 1986. "Confronting a traumatic event: Toward an understanding of inhibition and disease." *Journal of Abnormal Psychology* 95:274.

Poon, A., and S. Danoff-Burg. 2011. "Mindfulness as a moderator in expressive writing." *Journal of Clinical Psychology* 67(9):881–95.

Ramirez, G., and S.L. Beilock. 2011. "Writing about testing worries boosts exam performance in the classroom." *Science* 331:211–3.

Reblin, M., and B. Uchino. 2008. "Social and emotional support and its implication for health." *Current Opinion in Psychiatry* 21:201–5.

Reinhardt, J., K. Boerner, and A. Horowitz. 2006. "Good to have but not to use: Differential impact of perceived and received support on well-being." *Journal of Social and Personal Relationships* 23:117–29.

Schoutrop, M., Lange, A., Hanewalk, G., Davidovich, U., & Salomon, H. (2002). "Structured writing and processing major stressful events: A controlled trial." *Psychotherapy and Psychosomatics, 71,* 151-157.

Seligman, M. E. P., Steen, T. A., Park, N., & Peterson, C. (2005). "Positive Psychology Progress: Empirical Validation of Interventions." *American Psychologist, 60*(5), 410–421.

Sloan, D., Feinstein, B., & Marx, B. (2009). "The durability of beneficial health effects associated with expressive writing." *Anxiety, Stress, and Coping,* 1 (1–15).

Smith, T., J. Ruiz, and B. Uchino. 2004. "Mental activation of supportive ties, hostility, and cardiovascular reactivity to laboratory stress in young men and women." *Health Psychology* 23:476–85.

Smyth, J., Hockemeyer, J., & Tulloch, H. (2008). "Expressive writing and post-traumatic stress disorder: effects on trauma symptoms, mood states, and cortisol reactivity." *British Journal of Health Psychology,* 13(1), 85–93.

Smyth, J. M. (1998). "Written emotional expression: effect sizes, outcome types, and moderating variables." *Journal of Consulting Clinical Psychology,* 66(1), 174-184.

Spera, E.D., J.W. Buhrfeind, and J.W. Pennebaker. 1994. "Expressive writing and coping with job loss." *Academy of Management Journal* 37:722–33.

Stroebe, M., and H. Schut. 1999. "The dual process model of coping with bereavement: Rationale and description." *Death Studies* 23(3):197–224.

Suhr, M., Risch, A., & Wilz, G. (2017). "Maintaining mental health through positive writing: effects of a resource diary on depression and emotional regulation." *Journal of Clinical Psychology,* 73(12), 1586–1598.

Tedeschi, R.G., and L.G. Calhoun. *Trauma and transformation: Growing in the aftermath of suffering.* Newbury Park, CA: Sage, 1995.

Zhou, X., X. Wu, F. Fu, and Y. An. 2015. "Core belief challenge and rumination as predictors of PTSD and PTG among adolescent survivors of the Wenchuan earthquake." *Psychological Trauma: Theory, Research, Practice, and Policy* 7(4):391–7. https://doi-org.proxy-hs.researchport.umd.edu/10.1037/tra0000031.